SEARCHING GOD

SEARCHING GOD

An In-depth View Of Eight Writers

George Kuser
Author of Out of Kenya, Out of Istanbul

iUniverse, Inc.
New York Lincoln Shanghai

SEARCHING GOD
An In-depth View Of Eight Writers

iUniverse books may be ordered through booksellers or by contacting:

iUniverse
2021 Pine Lake Road, Suite 100
Lincoln, NE 68512
www.iuniverse.com
1-800-Authors (1-800-288-4677)

Because of the dynamic nature of the Internet, any Web addresses or links contained in this book may have changed since publication and may no longer be valid.

The views expressed in this work are solely those of the author and do not necessarily reflect the views of the publisher, and the publisher hereby disclaims any responsibility for them.

ISBN: 978-0-595-41693-6 (pbk)
ISBN: 978-0-595-86037-1 (ebk)

Printed in the United States of America

This book is dedicated to Mariane Kuser; we created our home in Italy from the earthquake's rubble, giving us the library and space to write.

Contents

Section Four: Psychology

A philosophical appreciation of books, both the reading and the writing of them, throughout life, and why I'm so indebted to the teachers I've studied with and to my children who have taught me so much.

Preface

Many decades ago, when I was in grammar school, I began reading the books that I write about here. I started writing about them twenty years ago, just before I moved my headquarters from Florence, Italy to Istanbul, Turkey. My academic mentor and long-time friend, Roy P. Fairfield, advised me to read Arnold Toynbee's twelve-volume *A Study of History*, the twentieth century's greatest book on history.

Years later, Roy suggested that he was writing a book about the one hundred most important books in his life, and suggested perhaps I should do the same. I narrowed the field to eight because I wanted to write more about each author and how they helped me grow and, think, and write. Many of my friends have read some of these books, but none of them have read all of them. I think this and I think that concept is important because each book you read and absorb becomes influential, in your own mind, influences you in peculiar ways owing to the connections between authors. In other words, I think differently today about Carl Jung, whom I read years before I read Arnold Toynbee, because Toynbee changed my thinking about Jung, and vice versa. I think this happens to every reader and writer. I think that readers will perhaps be encouraged to think of how these authors have altered their thinking, and how when they read authors they do not know, it might change their thinking about others they do know. It's a communication process between you and me as well as between you and yourself.

There are four general ideas I explore through these great writers: spirituality, history, mythology, and psychology. The book starts with a section on spirituality because without spirituality, a correct start in life is difficult. I use Kahlil Gibran's *The Prophet* because it had such a profound influence on my life at such an early age. As time has gone on, I have found Gibran's ideas to be an even more lasting influence than when I first read it.

The second section is "history," and I illustrate the wider sweeps of history through Arnold Toynbee's twelve-volume *A Study of History*, written in roughly the middle of the twentieth century. As we find ourselves at the start of a new century, we find contemporary examples of Toynbee's ideas, and explore his ideas in relation to religion. I use Toynbee's *An Historian's Approach to Religion* and his *Experiences* to build on what was written in his *Study*.

The third section, "creative mythology," was chosen because it is a core concept that contains ideas touching on all aspects of our lives. I explore the power of myth in society with Joseph Campbell, who was roughly a contemporary to Toynbee, and who, unlike Toynbee, explored the relationship between myth and religion. Campbell's many books on the subject were written in the middle to late twentieth century. *The Mask of God, Occidental Mythology,* and *Myths to Live By* are books I draw from most heavily, but other authors' works are included as well.

The last section I call "psychology" although it is really a psychological examination of aspects of mythology, and I chose three of the twentieth century's great psychiatrists, Carl Jung, Erich Neumann, and Carl Kerenyi, because they wrote so deeply and definitively about mythology.

I included Carl Jung in this section because he was an original thinker and writer on mythology, and his junior partner Erich Neumann because he was not merely well-trained by Jung but also developed original concepts of his own that are worth discussing. Jung's friend Kerenyi completes the trilogy. I use their various writings including books, essays, and jointly-written articles.

I think I'm attempting something rather easy here starting with Gibran's thoughts, but things get progressively more complex, or less simple, with Arnold Toynbee. The thoughts of the philosophers also begin somewhat simply with Joseph Campbell, but become more complex as life becomes increasingly complex for Jung and others. But the idea is that from this apparent complexity comes simplicity, and if you follow my words and thinking, you'll better understand what one life can strive for, and then match that up with what that life has become. This obviously has a therapeutic effect for me, allowing me to write about those matters that matter most to me, but I'm suggesting that anyone can do this, anyone can follow a plan of their own making for appreciating what they think is most important, then organize their lives to fit.

The eclectic approach I take within each section is a mirror of life, because each of us takes this approach, either on a daily basis or by taking a look at our own lives from an overall perspective. We can only read so much, and a nuclear physicist cannot spend the years with either Shakespeare or the authors I've cited that I and many, many others have. This book is about my choices of reading and their influence on me. It is both a path open to all and potentially satisfying to many.

Buona fortuna, as we Italians say.

Section One:
Spirituality

○ ○

To judge ourselves by our failures is to blame the seasons for their inconstancy.

—Kahlil Gibran

Chapter One
The Prophet and I

Introduction

Spirituality is the culmination of what we do with our lives, yet we need a spiritual direction at the start of life or we may get it all wrong. I begin this book with Gibran's *The Prophet* because it was an early and lasting spiritual influence on my life, but *The Prophet* includes more concrete ramifications, both in my life and the book because the concepts discussed there affect what we do in life.

I first read *The Prophet* when I was around seventeen, and I admired the poetry, thinking it vaguely romantic and quite suited to me. Later yet, I gradually acquired copies, some as gifts from parents and children. I keep one copy at my home in Italy, while I also carry one with me on my travels. I have underlined and starred various passages in most of the copies, and the passages underlined in later years tend to be more mystical. For example, the opening quote in this section about judging ourselves by our failures being like blaming the seasons for their inconstancy: that's an idea I would have passed by without really thinking when I was seventeen. Or twenty-seven or thirty-seven, for that matter. I simply didn't think of failure in those days, and when I did fail, I quickly pushed it out of mind, not wanting to admit to failure, but also not learning from it. I now know that understanding failure early on is both a spiritual leap forward and a step upward toward physical achievement, such as success in business or writing.

No other writing has held my attention for as many years as *The Prophet* has. My love affair with Shakespeare is also permanent and growing in depth, but I'd prefer *The Prophet* if I were stranded on a lonely isle with only one book, for Gibran has caught the seeds that have sprouted and flowered in my mind for over half a century, and a line from *The Prophet* can trigger my thoughts for an hour and more. Indeed, I know many of his phrases and can recall them from my memory as easily as from this computer's memory. Only, from my memory they come bearing gifts and ever-strange flowers that delight the mind and refresh the heart.

If you haven't read Gibran's *The Prophet*, I would suggest you do so. It is about a prophet who is about to depart, and he answers the questions posed by the people. The topics they ask cover the gamut of life, much as I've tried to do here. The chapter subheadings are mostly from *The Prophet* and are in the same order as Gibran presented them. I've added a few of my own after "Religion." In each subsection, I've tried to include details about how I have adapted Gibran's ideas to mine, or interpreted them. All the quotes are directly from Gibran. The idea is to set down a philosophy and whence it derives.

The Sea and I

Gibran's quote, "The sea that calls all things to her calls to me," must have left me cold sixty years ago, for I was not yet used to travel; I had yet to know that siren song beckoning to distant lands, different peoples, sounds, and languages. I missed this first reference to the sea then, but it's now an invisible thread tying the prophet to me because, like the prophet, I too embark on a spiritual journey to new lands. Even now, I'm amazed anew at how this prose has the simple power to move me.

I now know why I like rivers and frequently live by them: they are but reflections of my quest. The solution to life is the sea—after all, human life has a salinity similar to the sea. The sea is the container of the rivers, and by the rivers or the sea, I feel complete.

I lived for five years between the Black and Marmara seas. The short Bosporus connecting them is a river, as are the four that form it: the Danube, Dniester, Dnieper, and Don. I have visited and put my body in and wandered along the shores and wondered at all four of these rivers. The Bosporus is more than the sum of these four rivers, for it truly is alive with vitality and history and mist and decay, sometimes all at once, and I love it as though it were my soul. Gibran says "yet I know my soul is the sea," and I agree.

I feel especially connected to the Mediterranean, that wine-dark sea sailed over by all the great Homeric characters, from Ajax to Ulysses. And is not the Mediterranean Sea "my deeper dream become an awakening"? And shall I not now become a sailor, a person roaming the vast sea, our sleepless mother, finding there the peace and freedom that my rivers seek and find?

Much as the rivers cannot be contained and flow toward the sea, the apparently restless past sixty years have been a compulsion to look and to see and to feel everything, because to stay in one place would have been to crystallize, and be bound in a mold, the same as a coffin. I often dream of rest; not the rest of the coffin, but rather the rest of being where I belong, a place to think thoughts through for myself, as Gibran thought through for himself in *The Prophet*.

Love and Marriage

I've made so many mistakes in the name of love, yet the true idea of love was there for all those years and I could not, would not see it, except through the pain of experience; and is this not the message Gibran prophesies for us? I first thought Gibran's concept of crowning and crucifying as two parts of the same love only a poet's fancy, and dismissed it. How long does it take to learn this lesson? Some seem blessed with this knowledge at birth, and others never come to it, while I seem to have had to crucify others and myself before being crowned by this truth.

The secret is that love does indeed make you grow, but the pruning is just as important, for who can grow without it? Did not my first two wives prune me unmercifully? Yeah, both spiritually and financially, yet that pruning was necessary to my growth.

I was twenty-three when I was first married, and twenty-three is too young to appreciate any but the carnal aspects of marriage. Hence, I missed Gibran's idea of allowing space in our togetherness because I was rushing the pleasure aspect. I learned this while analyzing my apparent jealousy, for love has no room for jealousy. (Binding myself to wife one and then repeating the error with wife two is almost too much to chalk up to education. Immaturity is a more fitting word because it allows me to bypass harsher criticism, such as compulsive stupidity.) And really, in the first marriage, I only sought love's pleasure and peace. It did lead, long before its dissolution, to a containment of both my laughter and my tears.

Once again Gibran returns to the sea for the concept of allowing spaces, saying "Let it rather be a moving sea between the shores of your souls." A better command yet is to "Sing and dance together ... but let each of you be alone." Wives two and three were very strong on aloneness, and I am myself gradually sensing the importance of being alone. The concept of keeping alone time for oneself is especially important to me since I work at home for the most part.

Each of my wives has come to dread the sound of the keyboard, for how can I tell the muse when to visit? "If your muse arrives before eight am again, I'll kill her, and you too." Alone time is more than just removing myself from home from nine to five, for I'm often away for weeks at a time. I usually keep a diary of these travels, and I was amazed to see I spent more than six months away from home in 1990 following the fall of the Berlin Wall.

In the discourse about love, the prophet spoke about the difference between having God in your heart and being in His heart. Even those who don't believe in God know the difference between the two: the fullness of being within another's heart is the fullness of being. Remember the story about the young, poor couple who were tempted by a rich eccentric to starve for a week for money? At the end of the week, a crust of bread was thrown to them; the man tried to grab it to stuff into his own mouth, but was too weak. His wife took the bread and put it in his mouth. Love isn't selfish—it gives to another first because to give to itself is death.

Children

As father to seven children, I've always agreed with Gibran's concept of them being sons and daughters of life's longing for itself. However, life intrudes, and you must live with your issue or default on life. I believe now that children are, as Gibran says, indeed like arrows sent forth from my bow, and my children cannot be like me any more than I can be like them. It is true that "their souls exist in the world of tomorrow," which I cannot visit. But there are certain constraints I can exercise, such as more control over aspects of my children's children than either I exercised over my own children, or they can exercise over their own children.

This is a historical concept perhaps best realized in East Africa where they have ritualized it, giving a grandfather rights over his grandson that the father lacks and cannot interfere with.

I have a more modern example of just that concept. Homer was born and raised on a small farm near ancient Assos, Turkey, on the Aegean Sea. When he was ten years old, his parents considered his education complete and wished him to work on the farm with his father. However, Homer's illiterate grandfather, also named Homer, had grander dreams for his grandson and wished for him to attend boarding school. The school required entrance exams, and the parents agreed that if Homer passed, he could continue his schooling, but they also knew the competitive exams would eliminate him. Grandfather Homer appealed to my Turkish family and me to tutor Homer each day for the next six weeks. We did, Homer passed, and his grandfather had his wish answered.

What more can I say about children? Only this: when you have seven of anything, you need to spend time with each individual to compensate for the numbers.

Eating and Drinking

A meal without wine is a day without sunshine or a night without love. True passion is reflected in the way you eat and drink; do so like most Italians, and you are a passionate person.

Work

I agree with the prophet, who uses several examples to show that if work makes you happy and you love life because of your work, you are doubly blessed. I think about Michelangelo, when he found the shape of his own soul in a block of marble, who was not more blessed than the farmer who sings joyfully as he follows the plough, rejoicing in the fruitfulness he is creating. If you bake bread with thought and love, the bread is a joy to all who eat it and a double blessing to you, the baker. If you grow grapes and think of the soil and the places underneath where the taproot will search out the moisture and the flavors of the earth, then your wine will be blessed with flavor that ordinary wines do not have, just as the joyful baker's bread is superior to the fluffy stuff that has lost its flavor and goodness. Italians and American gospel singers make the best opera singers because they are raised from childhood to love their singing; it is a vital part of their lives, like breathing. What a difference between them and others who lack that inner love.

Joy and Sorrow

The deeper your capacity for both joy and sorrow, the greater your life, for you are measured by both. Those who suffer little, laugh, but not all their laughter, and those who have not tasted joy deeply may cry, but not all their tears. Joy and sorrow are inseparable from life because they are life.

Houses

Your house is indeed your larger body, as Gibran says, and if you lack harmony in your body or in your life, you can acquire it through building and living in a harmonious house. If your architect doesn't know Andrea Palladio, find another who does and ask them to build a home according to the principles of harmony Palladio set forth over four hundred years ago in his great *Four Books of Architecture*. Thomas Jefferson greatly admired Palladio and especially his Villa Rotunda just outside Vicenza, Italy. Jefferson copied that villa and built it anew in Virginia, calling it Monticello.

I built a combined house and office building in Troy, Ohio, some three hundred miles northwest of Monticello, also according to the principles of Palladio, some two hundred years after Jefferson built his. My Palladian design doesn't look anything like Monticello or any other Palladian building, for I wanted it to be the best of American design, yet according to Palladian principles.

Visitors exclaim, "What harmony, how beautiful!" It did not cost more than an ugly house would, but the architects, engineers, carpenters, and other workers all enjoyed working on this building because they could feel the inner harmony and beauty they were creating. This building is a better building because of their love expressed therein; those who sleep there claim a special peace pervades their slumber, and people tend to be happy within that house.

After buying a ruined stone house in Italy's Umbria, my wife Mariane and I redesigned and modernized (meaning central heating, a new idea in our village), raising the roof to put in modern anti-seismic devices, and then insulating against both cold and heat. Yet we still had a small house, until the 1997 earthquake killed so quickly in nearby Assisi and split our neighbor's adjoining house in pieces. He had to sell, so we bought, raising our 1,500 square feet to an ample 5,000. Our two houses were joined by a bridge and several common walls and contained a common courtyard with a magnificent view of the ancient castle below. It was a daunting challenge but also a great opportunity, and we spent almost three years redesigning the two houses into one. We started at the top, tearing off the damaged roof, then took the floors out and most of the walls down, but saved all the local stones to rebuild with. We changed the three floors into two, raised the roof and lowered the ground floor by digging down to bedrock, then slowly added infrastructure such as steel bands to avoid earthquake damage, then super insulation, plus under-the-floor heating. It was a daily inspiration, despite the dust and problems, for we were creating our own home out of virtual rubble, making it seem from the street to have never been different, just like the other sixty houses in our village.

Mariane and I had each built three or four houses before, but it was exciting to build this house together, also enervating but very satisfying. Five years after completion (is any house like this ever complete?), there are few changes we'd make ... the biggest change was putting ourselves into this house, making it a home.

In Gibran's words "For that which is boundless in you abides in the mansion of the sky, whose door is the morning mist, and whose windows are the songs and silences of night." A house is so much more than a place to hang your hat. When you build it in harmony with nature and with yourself, it becomes a place of repose. When you don't, as Gibran says, it can confine that which is boundless.

Why I Am Writing This

Now that you have read this far, you can see what I'm writing about; *The Prophet*, of course, but also my thinking, philosophy, and life according to Gibran's thoughts. Each chapter headline, except this one, is from *The Prophet*, and details how I have adapted Gibran's ideas to mine and interpreted them. All the quotes are directly from Gibran. The idea is to set down a philosophy and whence it derives. I think I'm attempting something rather easy here with Gibran's thoughts, but they get progressively more complex, or less simple, with Arnold Toynbee. The thoughts of the philosophers also begin somewhat simply with Joe Campbell, but become more complex as life becomes increasingly complex for Jung and others. The idea is that from this apparent complexity comes simplicity, and if you follow my words and thinking, you'll better understand what one life can strive for, and then match that up with what that life has become. This obviously has a therapeutic effect for me, allowing me to write about those matters that matter most to me, but I am also suggesting that anyone can do this, anyone can follow a plan of their own making for appreciating what they think is most important, then organize their lives to fit.

Clothes

"Modesty is for a shield against the eye of the unclean; the earth delights to feel your bare feet and the winds long to play with your hair." What a sense of longing I get when I see a naked child playing in the sand and sea. Cleanness is becoming childlike once more, and playing naked in the sun.

Buying and Selling

Gibran said "For the master spirit of the earth shall not sleep peacefully upon the wind till the needs of the least of you are satisfied."

I think the secret to operating a good newspaper or magazine, which is to think of your readers first, shows this principle. Every decision you make, ask yourself, "Will this be good for the readers?" Next you must think of your advertisers, for they pay your bills, and without both of them you are nothing. Then, your employees must be treated fairly, for if they don't like their work, the product will reflect it. Everyone's needs must be satisfied in order for it to be successful.

Crime and Punishment

Gibran says that wrongdoers are often mentioned as though they were not one of us, but as an illegal immigrant. But, he adds, the illegal intruder is driven by the hidden will of us all because no man is an island.

One of my first realizations of the above came after watching and studying Richard Wagner's *Ring Cycle* of operas, and identifying strongly with Wotan, the Norse concept of God. Only when Wotan has suffered can he appreciate the insight that he is not just a part of his enemy, Alberich, but he is "licht Alberich" himself. That is the crux of the entire cycle, the inner truth Wagner portrayed so well. Look in your heart, know your own soul before judging another.

Law

Gibran says that we delight in laying down laws, yet we delight even more in breaking them. Look around, and you too will see that this is true. Each time we break the law, we just add more laws.

In Gibran's words, "Like children playing by the sea who build sand towers with constancy and then destroy them with laughter. But while you build your sand towers the sea brings more sand to the shore, and when we destroy them the sea laughs with us. Verily, the sea always laughs with the innocent.

"But what of those to whom life is not a sea, and man-made laws are not sand towers, but to whom life is a rock, and the law a chisel with which they would carve it in their own likeness?

"What of the cripple who hates dancers? What of the dancer who hates cripples? What of the old serpent who cannot shed his skin and calls all others naked and shameless? What shall I say of these save they all stand in the sunlight, but with their backs to the sun."

Like those in Plato's cave allegory,
"they see only their shadows, and their shadows are their laws. For, what is the sun to them but a caster of shadows? What man's law shall bind you if you break your yoke, but upon no man's prison door? ... People of Orphalese, you can muffle the drum and you can loosen the strings of the lyre, but who shall command the skylark not to sing?"

Freedom

Gibran says that that which we call freedom is the strongest of the chains we bind ourselves with, though its links glitter in the sun and dazzle our eyes. He says that the chains are but fragments of our own selves that we discard to be free. For example, he tells us that if we would cast off a care, that care has been chosen by us rather than imposed on us. If we would dispel a fear, the seat of that fear is in our own heart.

Likewise, "if it is an unjust law you would abolish, that law was written with your own hand upon your own forehead." We cannot erase it by burning the law books nor by washing the foreheads of our judges, though through more litigation we may try!

And if it is a despot we would dethrone, we must first see that his throne within us is destroyed. "For how can a tyrant rule the free and the proud, but for a tyranny in their own freedom and a shame in their own pride?"

The communist tyrannies that had just begun as Gibran was writing *The Prophet* in 1923 are now shriveled and meaningless, but the story they reveal to those of us who have lived in Central Europe and the Soviet Union was accurately predicted by Gibran. Not only did the tyranny dwell in each of our hearts in order for a man such as Stalin to exist, but the damage to our collective psyche is only now becoming visible.

What a shock to live in Sofia or Bucharest, for example, and hear people today claim things were better under the tyrannies. The Bulgarian dictator Zhifkov, especially, is now looked on as something of a hero, and Bulgarians do not want the government to or think that the government will punish him. Zhifkov lives in many Bulgarians' hearts.

Freedom surely comes from the strength within.

Reason and Passion

Gibran writes that "your soul is oftentimes a battlefield, upon which your reason and your judgment wage war against your passion and your appetite." Reason and passion are the rudders and sails of our soul as we navigate the sea of life. "Reason, ruling alone, is a force confining, while passion, unattended, is a flame that burns to its own destruction."

"Let your souls exalt your reason to the height of passion, that they may sing, and let them direct your passion with reason ... When the storm comes and shakes the forest, and thunder and lightning proclaim the majesty of the sky, then let your hearts say in awe, 'God moves in passion'. When you sit in the cool shade on a forested hill, sharing the peace and serenity of distant fields and meadows, let your hearts say in silence, 'God rests in reason'.

"Since you are a breath in God's sphere and a leaf in God's forest, you too should rest in reason and move in passion."

Pain

Gibran writes that pain is the breaking of the shell that encloses our understanding. Much of our pain is self-chosen, for it is the bitter potion by which the physician within heals our sick self. Therefore, he says to trust the physician, and drink his remedy in silence and tranquility.

A paraphrase of his admonition: Welcome pain when it comes and clasp it to you, understanding the need, and pain will lessen and cease to upset, for it is natural. Sometimes pain is sent to test us or to act as a gateway to understanding, and then we must live with that pain and work our way through to new understanding, for this is life.

That may sound good and give some hope to truly hopeless cases, but in the eighty some years since he wrote these words our lives have become much longer, with many of us afflicted with pain as a constant companion. This kind of pain, usually a form of arthritis, can be depressing and even lead to suicide, making Gibran's brave words senseless or even insensitive. Better than words are the anti-inflammation drugs taken by millions daily that free many people from wheelchairs and beds, allowing them to walk normally and not appear as pitiable, decrepit seniors. Last year, my wife broke her back and the Italian doctor gave her a painkiller that lasted three days. While she was still in sanity-challenging pain, he intimated that she gaze at a crucifix to alleviate her pain.

I doubt whether that works for others here in Italy, but it certainly did not for my wife. Fortunately, I keep a sort of pharmacy here at home stuffed with cures one cannot find in Italy, such as Neurofen Plus, which is a lovely painkiller laced with codeine that is available over-the-counter in England. The point of the above words is that pain can be both physical and psychological, yet the former informs the latter.

A more explicit example of this is Joseph Conrad's *Lord Jim*. The idea that obsessed Joseph Conrad when he wrote *Lord Jim* in 1899 and 1900 was a curious version of honor, and Conrad deftly wrote how and why Jim had honor while the other Europeans with him did not. I could have titled this book *Lord George* because the heart of it is what Conrad wrote about and explained so well in his

Lord Jim, and I am as obsessed with this concept as Conrad was, but it is just as difficult for me to describe as it was for him. How to explain how and why one person has a certain trait, like honor or honesty, and a similar person does not?

While I was watching HBO late one night, *Lord Jim* suddenly appeared with a young Peter O'Toole cast as the protagonist. He seemed the wrong actor to play this character, who was nothing like a desert Arab or any of the other roles O'Toole has played. Then I recalled the paragraph in Conrad's book describing Jim, and I realized that any casting director reading that description would instantly think of Peter O'Toole, at least around 1960, with his blond hair, English good looks, and startlingly blue eyes. The movie is far easier to follow and understand than the book is, as some great movies are, but the central idea becomes clear through both media, and it is the moral question we all face and either avoid or resolve. Conrad makes it evident that avoiding the question is not without repercussions, for those who deny or reject morality seldom live happily thereafter. However, those, like Lord Jim, who face up to their moral obligations, may die for them. The result, according to Joseph Conrad, with which I agree, is that life is always placing demands on us, and if we wish to live a fulfilling life, meaning that we meet our own standards, we must be prepared to pay the price.

Pleasure

Gibran writes that "pleasure is a freedom song, but it is not freedom. It is the blossoming of our desires, but it is not their fruit. It is a depth calling to a height, but it is neither the deep nor the high. It is the caged taking wing, but it is not space encompassed."

Often we deny ourselves pleasure, and store the desire in the recesses of our being. Who knows but that which seems omitted today, waits for tomorrow?

"It is the pleasure of the bee to gather honey from the flower, but it is also the pleasure of the flower to yield its honey to the bee. For to the bee a flower is the fountain of life, and to the flower a bee is a messenger of love. And, to both the bee and the flower the giving and receiving of pleasure is a need and an ecstasy."

Yet some pleasure comes with a price: after an hour of love comes a lifetime of caring for a child.

Self-Knowledge

Gibran writes that our "hearts know in silence the secrets of the days and the nights," but our minds thirst for the heart's knowledge. We would know in words what we have always known in thought. We would touch with our fingers the naked bodies of our dreams, and it's well that we should. But we should not see and measure this treasure, for self is a sea boundless and measureless.

"Say not 'I have found the truth', but rather 'I have found a truth'. Say not 'I have found the path of the soul', but rather 'I have found the soul walking upon my path'. The soul walks not along a line, neither does it grow like a reed; it unfolds itself, like a lotus of countless petals."

The above quotes are all paraphrases of Gibran's thinking on self-knowledge, and the following is my summation of his thoughts. Some people, like Christ, Mohammad, and Buddha, must have exhibited several petals of their soul at an early age. Yet in a long life of searching for souls, mine and others, I've met many old ones with few petals, younger ones with none, and oldsters with both very many and very lovely petals, but never a young, many-petaled soul.

Why? Read on.

Teaching

"Nobody can reveal to you aught but that which already lies half asleep in the dawning of your knowledge ... The wise teacher does not bid you enter the house of his wisdom, rather he leads you to the threshold of your own mind. For the vision of one person lends not their wings to another."

My conclusion to Gibran's thoughts on teaching is the following. Think of the teachers you've had who really inspired you. How many are there? Maybe five, if you're lucky. Many of us go through life without knowing any. I consider myself fortunate in having two teachers who were, and are, not just great teachers who lead me to my own temple, but friends who shared their own passions and helped me to form my own. My indebtedness to Tom Yahkub of India and to Roy Fairfield of Maine, both from Harvard, runs far deeper than my academic roots. The only way to pay a debt like this is to devote my time and interest to other students, for the burden of being helped is to help others.

Friendship

"If I were to choose between betraying a friend or betraying my country, I hope I would have the guts to betray my country,." said E. M. Forster on a radio show in England in 1939.

Aristotle described luck as when your neighbor gets hit by an arrow directed at you. He wrote a lot about friendship, but never resolved the dilemma of having your friend killed by the arrow that might have hit you.

Gibran says that your friend is your needs answered, which sounds like a black joke in the preceding context, but is clarified thus:

"For, without words, in friendship all thoughts, all desires, all expectations are born and shared, with joy that is unacclaimed. And let there be no purpose in friendship save the deepening of the spirit. And let your best be for your friend; if they must know the ebb of your tide, let them know the flood also. For what is your friend that you should seek him with hours to kill? Seek him always with hours to live.

"For it is his to fill your need, but not your emptiness."

Talking

Gibran says that we talk when we cease to be at peace with our thoughts, and in much of our talking thinking is half-murdered. "For thought is a bird of space, that in a cage of words may, indeed, unfold its wings, but cannot fly."

There are those among us who talk through fear of being alone, for the silence of aloneness reveals to their eyes their naked selves and they would escape. And there are those who talk, and without knowledge or forethought reveal a truth which they themselves do not understand. Often I have thought of saying one thing, with my mind on another, and then something I hadn't thought of at all comes out. I treasure those phrases for frequently I feel as though they come from an inner depth I am out of touch with.

More and more we see and hear politicians who have mastered the art of talking and influencing others rather than expressing their own thoughts. But then there are those who have the truth within them, but tell it not in words.

"In the bosom of such as these the spirit dwells in rhythmic silence. When with your friend, let your inner spirit move your lips and guide your tongue. Let the voice within your voice speak to the ear of his ear, for his soul will keep the truth of your heart as the taste of the wine is remembered when the color is forgotten and the vessel is no more."

Time

Gibran says that we "measure time the measureless and immeasurable." "Of time we make a stream upon whose banks we sit and watch its flowing, yet the timeless in us is aware of life's timelessness, and knows that yesterday is but today's memory and tomorrow is today's dream."

Einstein showed us that perhaps time is compressible and even reversible, and that our universe is peopled with strange delights such as black holes that can suck in light and maybe even time till they cease to exist.

"If you must measure time into seasons, let each season encircle all the others, and let today embrace the past with remembrance and the future with longing."

Good and Evil

Gibran writes that "evil is good tortured by its own hunger and thirst; when good is hungry it seeks food even in dark caves, and when thirsty it drinks of dead waters. We are good when we are one with ourselves, yet when we are not one with ourselves we are not evil. For a divided house is not a den of thieves, it's only a divided house."

And being weak is not evil, it's only a lack of strength. When we do evil things through weakness, we are searching for good.

As an example, Kenya's natives in the first half of the twentieth century lived under colonial domination and were forced to be weak. In response, they reached into their dark cave of a past and brought forth a dead cat and called it Mau Mau. Yet the people who founded this movement were not evil; they were searching for good through the only channels open to them, and they found it.

Sometimes good or evil is a matter of perception. Kenya's natives won their battle against their colonial masters and are now considered to be heroes, but if they had lost that war, they would be known as terrorists instead of heroes.

"When we strive for gain we are but roots clinging to the earth and sucking at her breast. Surely the fruit cannot say to the root: 'Be like me, ripe and full and ever giving of your abundance'. For to the fruit giving is a need, as receiving is a need to the root." We are good when we strive to give of ourselves, yet we are not evil when we seek gain for ourselves. When we are not good, we are only lazy. In our longing for our giant self lies our goodness, and that longing is in all of us.

Beauty

We speak of many things when we speak of beauty, but mainly we speak of needs unsatisfied; and beauty is not a need but an ecstasy, according to Gibran. "Beauty is the image we see when we close our eyes, and the song we hear though we shut our ears. Beauty is life when life unveils its holy face. But we are life, and we are also the veil."

How often do we fail to see beauty—interior or exterior—because of what we think we behold? That's the veil Gibran talks about, and it is up to us to increase our awareness so that we can see the beauty around us, even in situations that might not appear beautiful at first.

Prayer

Gibran tells us "You pray in your distress and in your need; would that you might pray also in the fullness of your joy and in your days of abundance ... For what is prayer but the expansion of ourselves into the living ether?"

Often I find myself praying the memorized words learned in childhood, with no meaning attached to them as my mind wanders to strange fields or is numbed into inaction. But prayer can be a real effort to communicate with God and with our inner selves. Others call this meditation or dreaming, but if we allow our thoughts to dwell on a sorrow or a joy and invoke the help or thanks of God, this is prayer. The answer may come from within, but is this not God's way?

Religion and God

Gibran had "Religion" and "God" as two separate sections in *The Prophet*, but I have chosen to combine them here. Gibran has good things to say about both subjects, but I find that I have a lot more in common with Arnold Toynbee, who is discussed more in the next section of the book.

Gibran says that religion consists of all deeds and all reflections. "Who can separate his faith from his actions, or his belief from his occupations?" Our daily life is our temple and our religion.

"Look about and we shall see God playing with our children. Look into space and see Him walking in the clouds, outstretching His arms in the lightning and descending in rain. See Him smiling in flowers, then raising and waving His hands in trees."

I am peculiarly well qualified to discuss God since my series of marriages is somewhat unique: my first wife was a Christian, the second a Jew, and the third a Moslem. The religious hat trick, if you will. The interesting aspect of these Abrahamic religions is not their recognition of a single god, but rather their different approaches to it.

I was born a Christian, but early on I decided that there are things about Christianity that I could not accept, primarily the divinity of Christ. Islam is very comforting about this, for Christ is revered as a great prophet, and his mother Mary is sacred, but neither are accepted as divine.

For me, though I was an early lover of mythology and I could recognize the myth of Christ's birth of a virgin, I could not accept that part of the religion as a historical fact any more than I can accept the story of Adam and Eve as factual. But I do accept that Christ appeared on the earth as a prophet who preached one of the first expressions of love as God, or vice versa.

And I see love as the crux of Christ's teaching, for God, which is really just the concept of a higher authority, is inherent to mankind's love for their fellow man.

The explicit arguments Arnold Toynbee makes to these ends are best read in his book *Experiences*, written near the end of his long life, which explores the great ideas of mankind he'd thought and written about. Toynbee's creed, like mine, consists of a single sentence: "*Deus est mortale iuvare mortalem*," or that what most people call God is really just a human being helping another human.

When asked if I believe in God, my response is always a qualified yes, and the qualifier is quoted above.

Believing in this kind of God, and basing my practice of life on my thoughts on religion, I sum up my life by repeating that the only full life must be lived by helping our fellow human beings.

How can I say something like that after all the failures I've perpetrated on fellow humans? Ah, you're forgetting the opening words of this book: "To judge ourselves (and others) by our failures is to blame the seasons for their inconstancy."

Death

In the words of Gibran, "We would know the secret of death, but how shall we find it unless we seek it in the heart of life? If we would indeed behold the spirit of death, let us open our hearts to the body of life. The real truth is that life and death are one. Dying is being naked in the sunlight, and melting into the sun."

Age and Wisdom

From this point forward, I've added some of my own categories in the spirit of Gibran's prophet.

Age is refining. We constantly learn and grow and change and die. Those parts of ourselves that we cast away, or that wither and die, are natural processes at work. It is what we keep and keep growing that is important, not that which we slough off. Look not at our bodies and their withering, but exclaim in marvel at our minds and reflexes that constantly grow.

Who would trade his fifty-year-old mind for what he had at thirty, just to assume a more youthful body? (Faust? No, he kept his experienced mind.)

I love people, and talk with all ages, yet as quick as a bright thirty-year-old mind can be, it suffers by comparison with one twice that age that has been growing and winnowing and learning reflexes that no thirty-year-old could have.

D. H. Lawrence was thirty when he wrote *The Rainbow*. It's a brilliant book by a great writer, especially the chapter titled "Anna Victrix," which shows the love and strife between a man and a woman. It requires talent bordering on genius to write so penetratingly. If Lawrence had lived to be sixty, twice his age when he wrote *The Rainbow*, his performance might well have matched his promise.

Or consider F. Scott Fitzgerald's *This Side of Paradise*, which he wrote at only twenty-three! If he had only kept fulfilling his promise, and not lost hope, faith, and life, what might that genius have done? A partial answer to that question is Doris Lessing's *The Summer Before The Dark*, which demonstrates what a more mature Lawrence and Fitzgerald might have done. Born in 1919 when both the others were writing their genius out, Doris Lessing's talent flourished into maturity.

When does this growing and maturing process end? Only with death, for a mind that is constantly prodded to learn and to use that knowledge becomes better able to ponder that knowledge and to form wisdom from it. Talk with the brightest person under forty and you'll find interesting facts sorted out in newly fascinating ways and then used in a brilliant fashion. Yet, without that wisdom that only arrives with age, we are talking with a human computer. Wisdom, the factor of time plus experience plus a good mind, is what differentiates.

Giving of need is fear itself, and I agree that sometimes my well has indeed been full and yet my thirst has been great and unquenchable.

This point brings me to an inherent characteristic of mine: I need to give just as Gibran's trees and flowers need to give. I've known and felt this strongly, but never articulated it until my father died.

I began spending time with my mother then, and we explored the whole subject of wealth and giving. We found that my strange ideas were quite like my mother's, although she had never articulated them before because they were antithetic to my father's.

My mother gave with joy, and that joy is a part of her reward. Yet I give because I am compelled to give, much like a tree or flower. I, like them, would perish if I could not give; I would choke on my own unshared wealth.

Therefore my gifts are not worth praising any more than the gifts of flowers and trees, for I need to give my all.

Wealth

It has been said that we should give of ourselves so that worthy young people will be educated, and I agree, but I also feel that we should give of our created wealth so that wealth is recycled properly. I don't feel as though my wealth belongs to me; rather it is just in my keeping, and I am responsible for it being used or placed where it will do society most good, such as education.

My career created the wealth that educated my children and enabled them to choose other careers than mine. If my career had not been so financially good, would they have been able to choose another? I think this last question is improper to ask.

Is my societal and familial obligation to leave my children all the wealth I have created? I think not. My own children's needs have largely been met through their education. Trying to do anything more permanent is trying to control their lives beyond my grave, and I've seen that concept misfire in my own grandfather's, and others', cases too often to consider that approach.

Since wealth is in my keeping, yet belongs to society as a whole, I am clearly the person to say how and where and when I return it to society.

But how should I choose to return this wealth to society? I could make it over to some institution such as a school or foundation, but I've worked with a lot of people who operate these institutions and my personal disappointments with them leads me to prefer that they earn their monies themselves. By that, I mean that they should achieve excellence on a daily basis, and then should sell that excellence every year to their supporters.

I do not believe that institutions should have large portfolios of stocks, real estate, or whatever. A pile of money is a seductive thing for most humans, and educators and foundation managers are not exempt.

The institution that owns large amounts of money becomes lazy. Once again, this is human nature. I have looked at fund managers' waistlines, and there is a correlation between the amount of money in their care and their waist size. These fund managers will achieve more excellence (and be thinner) on a sustained basis of earning their yearly bread than they would through an endowment fund that encrusts their talent in easy money, luring it into a taste for comfort that is antithetic to excellence.

Should I give my money to a foundation that spends its own capital? Not a bad idea: an ad hoc foundation created to self-destruct within, say, twenty-five years. Ellen Stewart has used her La Mama Theater in New York informally to this end. She took her money from the MacArthur Foundation "genius" grant to purchase and restore a former grand house in Italy as an artist-in-residence and performing arts center. I have worked there, and it functions well. Will it continue to work a hundred years from now? Maybe. But it's better to partially fund it for a few years now and see how it functions. If it earns the right to raise enough funds to function, then it will be a continuing success.

I know that I don't have the full answer to the question of where and how to return my wealth to society, only an intimation of what is presently the best possible answer for me.

Meanwhile, there's nothing wrong, and a lot right, about enjoying spending money, something that both my mother and her favorite brother, Jim Kerney, taught me early on. I love Dom Perignon and caviar, but I've always followed my maternal grandfather's advice: "If you get a chance to spend a night on a yacht, grab it, for it's one of life's experiences. But don't get the yacht habit, for it's useless."

Fear and Courage

United States President Jack Kennedy defined courage as grace under pressure. I've been under pressure of many kinds, from a sudden accident to a prolonged intensity, and I have tried consciously to exhibit that sort of courage each time. But when you suddenly lose an engine at takeoff and must react instantly, no philosophy covers your "grace" period; you either react in a trained way or you suffer the consequences.

Another kind of pressure is physical confrontation. Too often have I faced down a fellow human, feeling cold and sick with fear, and then comes the rush of euphoria when the other person retreats. Is this courage?

I know a story that illustrates courage. A young pilot got married, fathered two children, and then went to war, where he shot down half a dozen enemy planes before he died. His widow married again, this time an older man who, after looking at his predecessor's photos in his home for many months, secretly took flight lessons and eventually learned how to fly solo. The evening he did so for the first time, he told his wife. Her comment was, "my first husband was without fear, and therefore he needed neither bravery nor courage to do what he did. But you are terrified of flying, yet you soloed. You have real courage, now please promise never to fly again."

So courage is really based on fear, and if we are afraid then we can either train ourselves to overcome it, or else develop a philosophy to do this. What appears to be bravery is often fearlessness, and if a person is fearless, they don't have courage for courage needs its counterpart, fear, in order to exist.

The Native Americans had a saying, "The brave man dies once, the coward a thousand times." I disagree with this because the "brave" man as defined in this saying is ignorant of fear, but the "coward" thinks of death frequently. For example, while driving a car, the coward sees a crash and his own mutilated corpse at every corner and over every hill, and therefore he drives more carefully.

Another example showing why courage and fear must appear together is in Richard Wagner's operatic hero, Siegfried. Siegfried, who is naturally stupid, is fearless and therefore without courage. He also lacks bravery, and this is one of the main reasons he screws up his relationship with Brunnhilda. He's ignorant of life; he lacks the basics and therefore doesn't understand love, only animal lust. If he had met Gudrun, his second interest, first, and worked out his lust on her, and then met Brunnhilda, he might have become a man. But as it was, he lived and died a child.

Curing and Blessing

"Will you be cured, or will you be blessed?" asks the saint of the lame man in Yeats's play *Beggars at the Waters of Immortality*.

"Cured" means having health, sanity, and insulation from life's mystery: a state of yin. To be "blessed" is to retain one's crippled status, one's history and memory of pain, plus the ability to share in a larger kind of life, such as dancing despite your lameness, and is a state of yang.

The real question of life is the following: do we prefer the apparent safety of a state of yin, or shall we risk all to be creative in a state of yang? Is it not a curse to be "cured"? Is not the curse of life to withhold one's blessing: the power to know and use what pain we must suffer?

Conclusion

As I said earlier, spirituality is the foundation of life because without it, life doesn't make much sense. The questions "Who is God?" and "Why am I here?" seem to have been pondered by humanity since the beginning of time.

Although I am comfortable borrowing Toynbee's definition of God as a human helping another human, I can't say I've yet reached a definitive conclusion about spirituality or about eternity. So like Gibran's prophet, I must set sail on the restless sea of discovery because to stay put is to wither and die.

I lived through three of the world's major religions: first as a Christian in New Jersey and Ohio, then as a Jew in New York City, and then as a Moslem in Turkey. This means that I have never effectively felt any social pressure, much less prejudice, to move me away from any of these religions. But neither have I been "religious" about any of these religions. This is an important distinction, especially when I talk with individuals who have come through tortuous experiences because of their religious life, such as Elie Wiesel.

Ultimately, we have to draw conclusions about truth and spirituality from within because the spiritual freedom we have dictates that we not only have the ability but also the duty to do just that.

What do I conclude from all this? Perhaps just that there is more to understand than I do presently.

Section Two:
History

o o o o o o o o o o o o o o o o o o o o o o o o o o o o o o o o o

Thought shall be the harder,
Heart the keener,
Mood shall be the more,
As our might lessens.

> —*"The Lay of the Battle of Maldon"*
> *Quoted by Arnold J. Toynbee at the opening of*
> *Volume One of* **A Study of History**

Chapter Two
Introduction

The first chapter of this book covered the spiritual aspect of life, whereas this next chapter covers the historical side. I rely on Arnold J. Toynbee and his writings, mainly his monumental *A Study of History* but also his other books, especially his last book *Experiences*, which was written in 1969 when he was eighty and aware that he was approaching the end of his creative life.

In the last two sections of this book, I use a group of mythological and psychological authors to complement and comment on the Toynbee works explained in this section. Largely, Toynbee and I have similar opinions of the authors in this category, preferring Jung to Freud for example. Toynbee wrote before Joseph Campbell did most of his work, so he does not refer to him, but Campbell would clearly be to Toynbee's liking; in preference, for example, to Edith Hamilton, Mary Renault, Robert Graves, or even Bullfinch. I think Toynbee would especially be pleased with Campbell's writings about Jung, and Toynbee would definitely approve of Campbell's concept of metaphor as both religion and myth.

I'll use the same framework here as in the earlier chapter, taking Toynbee's *A Study of History* subject by subject, subjectively. I'll discuss certain volumes but not all of them. Toynbee himself asked time and again "Why am I writing this?," and at the conclusion of his tenth volume, he included a section called "How this book came to be written." He obviously repeats himself in this inquiry, yet his method is valid, for he asks himself that question at varying periods of his work and his life, largely later on in both. His responses become increasingly more insightful, more personal, and not just useful to his books and readers but psychologically useful to Toynbee himself as he realizes that he, like history itself, is not a static wheel but a dynamic one, constantly growing and changing.

Toynbee, like me, wondered what "door of death" civilizations went through when they experienced their demise. His uses this as the reason why he devoted his life to history; although he always referred to it as "History," of course. Although this chapter opens the door to Toynbee's reasoning and soul just a crack, his last book, *Experiences*, leads the reader inside on a fascinating trip. I'll explore that book more fully at the end of this section, as it demonstrates to each of us readers how our own perceptions and dynamics change.

Chapter Three
The Exchanges of Civilization

Toynbee reviews about twenty-three major civilizations in the first volume of *A Study of History*, including the Egyptian, Andean, Sinic, Minoan, Sumerian, Mayan, Indic, Hittite, Hellenic, Western, Russian, Japanese, Orthodox Christian, Far Eastern, Iranian, Arabic, Hindu, Mexican, Yucatec, and Babylonian civilizations. I'm only going to focus on two, Hittite and Minoan, but facts about the other civilizations are woven in as I see fit.

My interpretation of Toynbee's introduction is that it serves a creative function for both the reader and more particularly for me. Much as I admire Toynbee, we have many differences, large and small. It sounds trite to say that he is a Brit and I a Yank, but those differing backgrounds go a long way toward explaining our basic differences. Anyone who grew up in a middle-class British environment roughly fifty years before I grew up in an American middle class has to be different from me. We lived in entirely different environments; for example, Toynbee's childhood was wrapped up in Queen Victoria's marvelous career, while mine was shaped by President Roosevelt's lengthy reign.

Toynbee was fascinated by languages and learned many, even writing poetry in Latin and Greek. His last wish was to have more time to study Turkish. His interest in pictographic writing and its successor cuneiform led him to learn those early forms. Toynbee delighted in looking deeply into the beginnings of religion, and described Christianity as a germ that was alien to the society in which it was founded, whereas Islam began as an indigenous germ. He did not comment on Judaism itself at this point, but it did start as a Syriac religion, meaning an indigenous one in this case, although it certainly became alien for thousands of years till it settled in Israel in 1948. It only appears to be living today in an alien world, for despite the hostility of its Arab neighbors, it is indigenous. So we can see that the three great Judaic religions all began in roughly the same area of the world, but while two were indigenous, Christianity was not, a point to keep in mind when reading Toynbee.

In Toynbee's introduction for the first volume, he demonstrates his never-ending process of looking at rather ordinary features in an individual and revolutionary way. To paraphrase his words: a frontier between a higher and a lower civilization is never stable, and usually the higher one is pushing the lower. However, when this higher pushing ceases, for whatever reason, the situation does not stabilize; rather, the lower civilization advances, and usually triumphantly.

An example of this is the ancient Hittite civilization. Toynbee didn't know much about the ancient Hittite civilization, because most of the information about it was only discovered and translated after Toynbee wrote.

I was living in Turkey in 1988 when I asked my teenage relatives Gulcin and Ali to study the Hittites during the school year. Then I took the two of them east to Turkey's capital, Ankara, and we spent our first two days in the magnificent archeological museum there, seeing first-hand evidence of these fantastic people from almost four thousand years ago. Then we drove east 150 kilometers to the ancient Hittite capital of Hattusas, leaving the paved highways further and further behind us as we passed over the Halys River onto a dirt track. We were already familiar with ancient Troy, on Turkey's west coast, for I had a summer home nearby, and we expected Hattusas to be as disappointing a sight as Troy is, but found instead that the glories of Hattusas far exceeded Troy's. Each day we explored a different part of this extraordinary mile-wide circular city, ringed with still-forbidding walls and towers.

The entrance to Hattusas is at its northern gate across the stream that flows by the eastern side of the city, but the city itself climbs far more steeply than the stream drops, perhaps rising over a hundred meters to the imposing southern gates. With what the archeologists have uncovered since 1988, the population of Hattusas could easily have been over fifty thousand people. A forgotten, or overlooked, empire with a capital city populated by fifty thousand stunned the imagination, especially when we drove north some thirty kilometers to the Halys River that was the dividing line between the Hittites (civilization) and the Gasga (barbarians). Those barbarians lived up to their name because almost no relic of their civilization remains today, yet they constantly picked at the Hittites, especially when Hattusas was relatively empty with the army away on some expedition.

How did the lowly Gasga manage to eat away at the lordly Hittites to the point where they disappeared? Was it a sudden bursting of their "impregnable" walls? I doubt it, for their strongholds, especially in the Taurus Mountains, were apparently used in later years precisely in order to escape the barbarians. I wonder about all the other influences on the Hittites, as we only saw about one third of their empire that summer.

The following January, however, my two young relatives and I were in the southeast of Turkey and I wanted to show them Carchemish, a past and current outpost on the Euphrates river where it crosses into modern Syria. The young Turkish lieutenant in charge of the military outpost there was most anxious to talk with us since no tourists ever visit, and it is a very isolated part of the desert. I asked him about his studies in military history and he was eager to tell me all about them, but they only began with Ataturk's Battle of Gallipoli less than a century ago. I returned his story with another, only mine was about a battle near Carchemish some 3,200 years ago. The Hittites ruled most of this area as the dominant force then, and they called in all their own armies, plus those of kings who owed allegiance to them, to fight the Egyptians under their Pharaoh Ramses II.

Tales of that battle, at Kadesh in the Bekaa Valley of present-day Lebanon, has been translated from the cuneiform blocks of clay as a total rout of the Egyptian force. The defeated Egyptian army crept home, and somewhere along the way Ramses decided that the only way the Egyptians would know about the battle was to re-invent it as a triumph, which he did, including a huge depiction of himself shooting the enemy cut into the rock building on the Nile River. Historians only saw his side of the battle, and decided it must have been a great victory for Ramses. This is one of the earliest instances of distortion becoming "fact," a practice we humans have since polished.

Minoans not what Toynbee Thought

Toynbee also explored the Minoan civilization, concluding mainly that they were superseded by the Greeks. The discoveries concerning the Minoans since Toynbee wrote make them out to be far more fascinating than he imagined. Recent work suggests that the Minoan society died suddenly. Toynbee knew intimately the myths concerning Theseus and the Minotaur, followed by Daedalus and son Icarus departing the same island, but he did not know why the Minoan civilization crumbled.

I spent the summer of 1978 trying to find the answer to the question of the demise of the Minoans by living in most of the archeological areas involved. Crete was the most interesting, for the Minoans lived almost exclusively on this island, and there are many ruins that they left behind that are still uncovered, such as the easternmost part of Crete, Zakros. This area was just beginning to be worked on in 1978, and the dust and ashes from the explosion of nearby Thera's (now Santorini's) volcano over three thousand years ago are still evident and, in some places, look recent. The falling ash must have been deadly, as it was over a millennium later in Italy's Pompeii. But the real damage would have been done by the giant tsunami resulting from Thera's explosion.

Since the volcanic explosion took place just below the surface of the sea, the resulting wave is estimated by geologists to have been over forty feet high. Even a wave half that size would have been sufficient to wipe out not just the port of Heraklion, but also the Palace at Knossos just south of there. Since it arrived without warning, it would have caught people, ships, and commerce with no adequate defenses. The destruction must have been greater, in terms of society, than the atom bombs dropped on Japan. Even if the Minoans were ascendant, their society would have been destroyed, smashed back to precivilization in a catastrophe we can only imagine.

The same summer that I was marveling at the destruction on Crete, I took a ferryboat across the Aegean Sea to the origin of the disaster on ancient Thera. It's worth a long detour just to arrive via boat inside the crater, and then to mount the steep sides of that crater via donkey to the rim, where I stayed in a tiny inn for three days. The real glory of this tiny island-crater is still underground: the magnificent ancient city of Akrotiri, preserved, as was Vesuvius's Herculaneum, by the lava that washed over it, freezing it like a fly in amber.

They were just starting work on Akrotiri when I visited in the summer of 1978, yet already you could see the outlines of what they would uncover, and wonder at the state of preservation of so much detail so close to the epicenter of the disaster. Today, more than thirty years later, I read avidly about this site, hoping to return and see the marvels rescued from the lava.

Co-invention of the Wheel

Toynbee next introduces J. Murphy and quotes him and others about the similarity of human thoughts and developments in different places at the same time; in short, the co-invention of the wheel. He cites as an example the similar intellects of Darwin and Wallace, who came up with remarkably similar theories of evolution at the same time. I think that historical circumstances are mainly responsible as prime movers of intellect. For example, both Darwin and Wallace were the same age, lived in the same small country, probably read the same newspapers, and shared the same education. In effect, they were probably equally smart, equally exposed to the same stimuli over a long period of time, and then they developed equal interests. It really is not surprising they came to the same conclusions.

The Value of Fiction

Toynbee's conclusion in volume one is that histories, such as the *Iliad*, need to use fiction. He neglects to mention that all religions need the same element of fiction to survive. Indeed, throughout his *Study* he frequently bends his knee to religion, in particular the Church of England. Only in his last work, *Experiences*, does he come out of that closet, telling us he had not in fact just recently decided to be agnostic, but rather had been one since the age of seven.

How can we reconcile his innate honesty with so many obeisances to religion throughout *A Study of History*? I suggest that, for Toynbee, the times demanded obedience to the culture, and those times were demanding because they were tough: in the midst of the Great Depression, Toynbee was financially secure with a job he loved and wanted to fulfill. Why should he endanger his lifework with an outburst against the morals of the time and wind up unemployed, unemployable? I think he overdid it a bit, but I don't blame him.

Toynbee's concept of needing fiction came home to me several years ago when a good friend was murdered. I mentioned this to my friend and academic mentor Dr. Roy P. Fairfield since he also knew the murdered man. Roy suggested to me that the only way for me to resolve the murder to my own satisfaction was to write about it fictionally. This was a new idea to me, and I explored the idea at length and in depth. I even discussed it with the slain man's widow, seeking her help and access to all her data on her husband's murder. She somewhat startled me by enthusiastically agreeing, then commenting that she would like to help write the fiction. Like so much in real life, I could not accept her active help for reasons I could not explain to her, although I did discuss them with my lawyer, who was also her lawyer, and the discussion between me and the lawyer became a telling of secrets on both sides. The matter was becoming a scene from Kafka when the law entered as a small-town sheriff with no previous work on matters criminal solved the murder.

After that experience, I began researching the ancient Hittite civilization which had far more intriguing blanks because of the over three thousand years that had elapsed since they existed. I decided to write a novel about them while I was living in their land, exploring their cities and art, and the words flew from my pen. When I rewrote that novel, I realized that it answered a lot of my questions about the Hittites, but that it was a lousy novel.

Two years later I was back in Hattusas, the Hittite capital, and met the German archeologist in charge. I told him I'd been there and bribed the guard to let me see the royal tomb the archeologist had discovered.

I asked him what had happened since my last visit, and he told me a strange story as we walked to the ancient royal tomb. We admired the reality, complete with carvings telling exactly who the ruler was and what he had done in life. We both knew who the king was, and next we admired his portrait, engraved in the stone of the "door." "What was inside the tomb," I asked. "Nothing" replied the archeologist. He waved at the three-hundred-plus Turkish workers digging out a magnificent wall leading to the tomb, a discovery worth a summer's labor for sure.

The German was both mystified and unsatisfied. "What use is this beautiful wall when I have nothing, almost nothing, in this tomb?" He dug to the bedrock behind, where the body and riches should have been, then fanned out to the sides. Nothing. The only alternative was straight down. He dug, and there, under the heavy stone door, was another large stone, but this one stated solemnly, in Hittite "This is the way to Hell."

Time was up for that archeologist for that summer, and all he could do was dream until next summer. My suggestion to him was to try writing a fictional account, opening his imagination to all possibilities.

Carl Jung would reply that the series is the context which the dreamer himself supplies. I replace "dreamer" in this context with "writer" or "fictionalizer." Jung concludes that we cannot control our own consciousness. I disagree, suggesting that we can fictionalize irreconcilable events, and thereby influence the unconscious; in effect, meddle with it, and hasten its process to yield a solution.

Chapter Four
Genesis of Civilization

In the second volume of *A Study of History*, Toynbee discusses the genesis of civilizations. Toynbee's first law of genesis and growth is that imitation is directed toward creative people because they are pioneers. Custom is broken and "society is in dynamic motion along a course of change and growth." I quote myself, writing in 1992:

> This has great meaning today as Boris Yeltsin pioneers where none have trod before. I believe that Yeltsin will have more supporters than detractors if he can survive the economic shakeout. That's tantamount to saying whoever goes over Niagara Falls in a barrel will be famous if he lives, yet Yeltsin has a much better chance of survival than either the fellow in the barrel, or the fellow who started it all: Gorbachov. Mimesis is hard to practise when you're starving, with less to eat than a year ago, yet I believe Yeltsin has the strength of character and charisma to incur mimesis among the Russians, where Gorbachov failed. First, Yeltsin saw the need for a democratic base in this new ballgame, and seized one, while Gorbachov held back, and lost … Yeltsin next seized more power, a strategem necessary to resolve and perpetuate his present, although it could equally threaten his future.

In 1990, I was driving through Russia at the same time as Yeltsin was touring his country. Tataria, the home of the Tatars, is in the far eastern part of the country, and Yeltsin's visit was tumultuous for the Tatars and especially their elected officials. "We have too many Russians here, and only two per cent speak our Tatar language." "We want to secede from the Soviet Union [Russia] and become sovereign." How did Yeltsin respond to these questions, to this problem? Remember how Gorbachov responded to the Lithuanians in March of 1990, then listen to Yeltsin address a group of Tatar intellectuals: "We don't want to make the same mistake [that Gorbachov did] in suppressing the urge to independence."

He went on to make it clear to these strongly secessionist-minded intellectuals that he, as chairman of the Russian Republic, would support Tataria's sovereignty in every way possible." "The surprised response of the elected Tatar officials is refreshingly open and open-minded. Many of them feel, after Yeltsin's visit, that he represents their best hope for independence, meaning they would like to be out of the Soviet Union, but they now think they prefer to remain in Russia itself." "We think the sovereignty issue should be postponed for two to three months. In the meantime, we should do some hard work before putting the issue to a referendum."

"Asked by a Moscow News reporter if they had changed their minds and thinking because of Yeltsin's visit, they replied: 'Yeltsin elicits confidence.'" "We have to think it all over." "One of them summed up the feelings of most of these local officials: 'Yeltsin is a charismatic person and many people liked him here.' Many people were relieved to hear him repeat these words in many of his speeches: 'It's up to you to decide your future.'"

Two years later, Yeltsin had strengthened his own position as well as that of Russia, and Tataria was still a part of Russia. But the real question then was what happened to communism? Joseph Campbell, the mythologist who I will write about in the next chapter, would answer that any society that treasures and keeps its myths alive will survive. Communism killed the old myths off, and tried to substitute their own. This failed because the strategy ran counter to human nature, resulting in the sad spectacle today of forlorn crowds marching in the first May Day parade after the fall of communism, yet still marching for communism as it was their only belief, their only myth. They were "nourished from the weakest, poorest strata of the human spirit," as Carl Jung put it.

Jung suggests that the only recourse that these outcasts have today is to start a dialogue about symbols from the unconscious interacting with the conscious. Good luck.

Yin and Yang

Toynbee considers that 98 percent of mankind's existence has been spent in a yin phase, largely static, and has only recently moved to the yang phase, which is dynamic. This is a core concept of Toynbee's, and of my own. Toynbee asks "what caused mankind to go from yin to yang?" His conclusion is that the future we search for is not an entity but a relationship, and this relationship could be between inhuman forces or between two strong, maybe superhuman, personalities. He illustrates with references to Yahweh and the Serpent, and the Lord and Mephistopheles in Goethe's Faust, while I prefer to interpret it as the conflict between Wotan and Alberich in Richard Wagner's operatic *Ring Cycle*.

I review Harold Bloom's 2006 book *Jesus and Yahweh: The Names Divine* in the bibliography later on, but Bloom's thinking is apt here. He suggests considering and discussing a comparison of Jesus and Yahweh to characters from Shakespeare, with Jesus as Hamlet and Yahweh as Lear.

Myth has played a dominant role in my life, as it has in many others, yet I was seventeen before I learned the difference between myth and historical fact. I realized then that I simply could not accept the virgin birth of Jesus Christ as historical fact, even though I can accept that he was born, as most historians do. I went through the entire Christian mythology then, realizing I could not accept most of it as historical fact. Yet it required years before I understood that human nature and religion require myth in order to exist. The failure of the Christian churches to confront this problem, and their stubborn insistence that all Christian myth is historical fact, is their greatest weakness, their "historical" weakness, albeit one also shared by both Jews and Muslims.

Dostoevsky illustrates the heart of the matter in chapter five of *The Brothers Karamazov*, "The Grand Inquisitor." In this chapter, Christ returns to earth in Spain during the early Inquisition, and winds up being tried before the Grand Inquisitor himself. Their discussion results in the Grand Inquisitor admitting to Christ that He is Christ, but the heart of the matter is that he must kill Christ because He is Christ.

Toynbee illustrates the presence of a modern theory in a long-ago myth by quoting Sir James Jeans:

> We believe ... that some two thousand million years ago ... a second star, wandering blindly through space, happened to come within hailing distance of our sun. Just as the sun and the moon raise tides on the earth, so this second star must have raised tides on the surface of the sun. But they would have been very different from the puny tides which the relatively small mass of our moon raises in our oceans; a huge tidal wave must have travelled over the surface of the sun, ultimately forming a mountain of prodigious height, which would rise higher and higher as the star came nearer and nearer. And, before the second star began to recede, its tidal pull had become so powerful that this mountain was torn to pieces and threw off small pieces of itself, much as the crest of a wave throws off spray. These small fragments have

been circling around their parent ever since. They are the planets, large and small, of which our earth is one.

Toynbee commented on this sun show by suggesting that this was the origin of the ancient myth about the sun god and its ravisher, a myth he claims is known to all primitive, or illiterate, peoples. I spent five years researching among dozens of tribes such as the one in Kenya, and have never heard this myth mentioned, although it sounds reasonable to me. Furthermore, in these myths civilization is presented with a series of problems. Each problem is a challenge to undergo an ordeal, requiring a response. In each case the story begins in a state of yin. As an example, Faust is perfect in knowledge, and what could portray the concept of yin better than the opening chords of Wagner's opera *Das Rheingold*?

Yin is brought to a state of yang through outside change. This can come from almost any outside factor, such as the Serpent in Genesis, Mephistopheles in Faust, or Loge in Wagner's *Ring*. Mythologically, Toynbee continues, yin passes over into yang because the devil intrudes into the universe of God. Only myth can explain this example of God's limitation.

I see Wotan, as portrayed by Wagner, as an obvious example of this intrusion, and I personally identify with this character, as do many others. Wotan's challenger, Alberich, may be foredoomed to failure, as Mephistopheles is in Faust, yet Wotan is not sure of success either. The essence of Wagner's *Ring Cycle*, like life itself, is the uncertainty of the outcome, even after the final curtain.

The clean, clear victory of either Wotan or Alberich, of light or darkness, good or evil, is never achieved either in Wagner's operas or in life itself. Wagner's own life was a series of personal disasters, and only his musical genius transcended them. Wagner and his *Ring Cycle* were not known to Toynbee, but they have been an integral part of my life for thirty years, and I believe that others who know the world of Wagner's operas can appreciate the comparison.

Another example of the transfer from yin to yang is evident in the natural world. Many thousands of years ago, the present Sahara Desert and Syrian Desert were lush grasslands. Indeed, the Syrian Desert may have been the original Fertile Crescent. The gradual desiccation of both these areas gave rise to the Egyptian and Syrian civilizations. Both of these civilizations were created through the process of people changing both their habitat and their way of life, suggesting that this double reaction was the dynamic cause of civilization in both cases. In other words, these two peoples existed in a state of yin among the lush grasslands, and only the increasing desiccation forced them to the radical response of draining swamps, building dikes, and becoming settled agriculturalists, which is yang.

A third example of this change from yin to yang is found in Homer's *Odyssey*. Odysseus was more in danger from Circe than he was from Cyclops. Although Circe was divinely fairer than Odysseus' wife Penelope, she was also inhumanly inferior as a helpmate for a mortal. (Sounds like the story of my life.) One conclusion I've learned is to welcome the "Cyclops" challenges for they are less dangerous than the "Circe" ones.

In addition to discussing the sun myth as closely related to scientific theory, Toynbee also comments on Charles Kingsley's myth of wind-direction preference as a cause for devolution. He introduces Charles Kingsley as "that Victorian exponent of the strenuous life who preferred the northeast wind to the southwest one." Toynbee quotes Kingsley as creating a myth showing that those who prefer the southwest wind degenerate into gorillas; what would Darwin make of that?

Challenge and Adversity

Toynbee sums up, in what I term his First Law of Civilization, how civilizations respond to challenges and adversity: ease is inimical to civilization, and the more difficult a challenge is, the more creative and greater the response will be. There are many sources of these challenges; for example, Toynbee discusses five environmental challenges faced by civilizations: hard countries, new ground, blows, pressures, and penalizations.

For me, the most difficult challenge in my life was being forced out of my assured yin life at the age of twenty-eight. This was involuntary, due to an external stimulus: I was fired and had three months to find another job, with three children under three years of age, a wife, and a mountain of debt.

I was writing the above paragraph in 1992 when a knock at the door brought an old friend who sought my help in the largest challenge in his life. Nicki was a man I had met in Tbilisi, Georgia, several years before, a sort of underground economy master of the area at the age of thirty-eight. Since our first encounter, the Georgian civil war had erupted and he had lost his power, his wife, and his son, all at once. He arrived at my home in Istanbul with about three U.S. dollars in his pocket, and no claim to the future except his knowledge of my address. He accepted the end of the yin part of his life, and rose to the yang, with a little help from me.

Toynbee cites many examples of challenges being met, but his favorite, because it fits all his criteria, is the story of the ancient Jews and Israel. After examining examples of civilizations that responded to challenges by moving geographically (in other words, forging new ground), Toynbee adds a clause to his

Law of Civilization: "new ground provides a greater stimulus than old ground." He adds to this that a sea-crossing has a stimulating effect, which to me sounds like an advertisement for a cruise ship.

Progressing from Toynbee's Law to his amendments quoted above, we arrive at his "formula": drama develops at home, whereas epic develops among migrating people. He next examines other stimuli than those relating to geographic location, such as external blows, external pressures, and internal penalizations.

The concept of "stimulus of blows" reminds me of a strange Canadian film I saw, *Black Robe*, about the Jesuits in the early days of their exploration of Canada, and the incredible hardships they faced. The protagonist "Black Robe" receives real blows from the Huron Indians who captured him and tortured him, along with the Indians who had been helping him, before tossing them into a hut for the night and planning to kill them the next day. After their miraculous escape that night, "Black Robe" goes on to live with other Huron Indians even further west, meeting challenge after challenge without progressing either materially or spiritually, until the final challenge when he is killed.

The implication is that a severe enough string of blows, combined with the stimulus of daily pressures, can seriously weaken the strongest person until they have nothing left with which to meet the next challenge, and they perish. The probable moral Toynbee would draw from this film is to reach for the stars but make sure that you have your feet on the ground. He would also probably cite the natural law of excess, meaning that nature makes an excessive number of most things so that a million can fail, but there will be at least one left over to succeed.

By the "stimulus of penalization," the final stimulus, Toynbee refers to the existence of lame smiths and blind poets, those who surmount physical affliction and achieve great things despite this constant internal penalization. I can only hope that I'd have the strength to develop in this way if so afflicted.

Slavery is something else, and perhaps easier to empathize with because it can be temporary; or maybe because we've all thought about it and seen the effects of it.

Toynbee expresses horror at what civilization inflicted on Africans and on itself through slavery. It is the most demeaning thing that mankind has done to itself, and I can see no good arising from the "stimulus" of slavery. Toynbee takes a longer view than I, and suggests that the American Negro Church could be seen as the dynamic response to slavery. I agree that it could, but I don't see any individual catalyst of response since the death of Martin Luther King.

I wrote the biography of James Gichuru, Kenya's minister for finance, and I came to know him well during the years we worked together. We had to trust each other, for I wanted him to unburden his soul and mind to me and tell me how and why he founded the secret Mau Mau Society. The external pressure on James Gichuru, and most of the other millions of native Kenyans, amounted to almost slavery, and was certainly a deprivation of their human dignity. None of them had any legal or physical means to combat their oppressors, the British colonialists who were present in Kenya from 1904 to 1952, so Gichuru reached into the dark recesses of his ancestral past and brought forth a dead cat and called it Mau Mau.

The result of his response to the challenge was freedom, "Uhuru" in Swahili, and it came about within less than a decade, with fewer than a hundred white colonialists being killed.

We are attempting, however, to understand the processes by which civilizations and individuals respond to challenges, and a situation of excessive pressure, such as slavery, doesn't seem to elicit the creative response that something short of it does. Toynbee mentions the "prodigality of nature," the natural excess that I referred to above, but I think that this concept is unreasonable, especially if you offer it as a hope to somebody suffering under what appears to be endless domination.

Chapter Five
Growth of Civilization

In the third volume of *A Study of History*, Toynbee discusses the growths of civilizations, giving examples of the arrested civilizations of the Polynesians, Eskimos, and nomads. Extreme climate can prevent a civilization from developing, as the Eskimos demonstrate. Toynbee asks whether the Eskimos are masters or slaves of their harsh environment. Based on the analysis in the previous chapter, we can say that the optimum challenge is one that provokes a response that goes further than a single move and becomes instead a concerted effort, facilitating the transition from yin to yang.

There is growth both in the macrocosm and in the microcosm. Macrocosmic growth is a progressive control over the external environment, whereas microcosmic growth is inner, revealing itself as self-determination or self-articulation. For an individual, macrocosmic growth would be the acquisition of power within a community or company, and microcosmic growth would be growth within oneself.

Toynbee asserts that geographical expansion is not a criterion of true growth of a civilization. In situations where it appears that geographical growth is real growth, this is merely a coincidence. It is more common for geographical expansion to coincide with a time of troubles, a stage of decline and disintegration. Why? Because troubled times make for militaristic solutions, such as recent actions in Afghanistan, Iraq, and Israel-Palestine. And these military solutions lead inevitably to the breakdown of civilization.

Another example is the Minoan civilization. As the Minoan state went into deep decline, all the material products of their culture became artistically inferior, just as their distribution became geographically superior. Toynbee sees application of the above to our present Western civilization, raising a question mark here which he only answers later on.

To explore the process of individual growth, Toynbee cites Shakespeare, giving as examples Henry V, Macbeth, and Hamlet. He sees Henry V as a young hero who is living on the outside of himself, a primitive youth, whereas Macbeth is equally divided between his inner self and his outer self, and Hamlet is totally absorbed within himself.

In conclusion, a social body tends to develop from outer influences toward inner ones. Toynbee has some startling thoughts that can be applied to the 1990s though he wrote them in the 1930s, sixty years before, saying that Communism developed from western sources (Karl Marx lived and wrote in London), showing how powerful western civilization is.

Self-Determination

Toynbee predicted that the West would win over communism in the end because Western civilization was based on self-determination whereas communism was not. What is self-determination? It is a constant state of inner yang. A concatenation of creative growth. To define it negatively, it is a denial of the state of yin.

My life has been full of a yearning for yin, foreswearing yang because I haven't thought through most challenges, nor do I adequately consider my responses. Like most, I've always wanted wealth and power. To achieve that longing is yin, and it may not be sin but it sure is the decay of ideation, of creativity, and of growth.

One of my favorite people was Emil Soubrey, an English gentleman with a French name who was a fine person. Emil entered my life when he was eighty and I was fifty—a generation apart. The twinkle in his eye alone endeared him to me, but his conversation was also so lovely, so intelligently creative! And then I learned his story, how he'd grown up in Europe until he became the head of Esso Europe, a big job. Emil's best friend was the same age, and he became head of overall Esso, later Exxon. They worked together and they retired together, but Gene Holman could not relax or adjust from his macrocosmic job to his microcosmic life, and he died.

Whereas when Emil retired, he changed his whole life in order to adjust to a microcosmic new one, marrying his friend of many years, and buying a flat in New York for them to spend their winters in, attending theater and opera and meeting new friends and enjoying the inner life. On the first of April each year, they left the fools behind and sailed on the *Queen Elizabeth* to France and their cottage in Cannes, nestled among lovely rocks and flowers with a view of the Mediterranean Sea.

I stopped by their cottage one May or June to take them to lunch at one of the great restaurants nearby, and Emil suggested we drink a few bubbles first, to "clear our palates and our minds for some serious eating and conversation." Emil lived life so fully that his widow went into a real depression when he died, at age eighty-five, brimming over with a life lived to the full. Yes, Emil Soubray represents a life lived fully, a mature self-determination.

Self-determination is also self-articulation, or knowing who and what you are and being articulate when explaining yourself. It's maturity and discipline, too, and perhaps the best one-word definition is "happiness."

Creative Members of Society

Toynbee knew that civilization defines itself through its individual members. Those who are creative reach civilization's highest plane. I can follow the action phases of my life as well as the ecstasy ones, but those active phases don't always work out well for me. For example, the "action" of working for the *Washington Post* was on a new and higher plane for me, but it was not a satisfactory one. I was distinctly unhappy working for such a large company which reminded me in many respects of the U.S. Army. I left there and went to the Metropolitan Opera, and while I loved opera, that was not enough to cover the fact that the Met was a big company and I was being squeezed by them even more impersonally than in the Army or at the *Post*.

Let us return to Toynbee and his description of Plato's allegory of the cave. He analyzes this allegory at great length, concluding that we cannot just be passive members of society but rather must be active. I have agreed wholeheartedly with this concept since my freshman philosophy course. Even when I succeed in becoming microcosmic, I feel compelled to exercise that success in the active world, which is the reason I was working at the Metropolitan Opera.

Toynbee cites Muhammad as an example because at his time (AD 570–632), Arabia had neither monotheism nor law and order. Muhammad instilled his vision of monotheism and law and order into his society, and it became Islam. Toynbee also cites Machiavelli as the creator of the seeds of western political philosophy. I have long admired Machiavelli, partly because I was a Florentine for over a decade and read his works in situ. I came to empathize with him to the point where I'd like to borrow his epitaph, *"Ha pisciato in tanto neve."*

Toynbee next speculates that Russia may be ready to return to Western society in a creative role. Strange words, written prophetically half a century before they started becoming true in 1992. Toynbee sums up this section on the growth of civilizations by saying that growth is achieved when either an individual or a society replies to a challenge by raising the stakes, so that the action proceeds to a higher plane.

Chapter Six
Breakdown of Civilizations

Toynbee discusses the breakdown of civilizations in volume four, largely focusing on the failure of self-determination as the cause of such a breakdown. Breakdown is more obvious than growth. It is a loss of creative power in individuals, divesting them of their power to influence others. As a creative minority degenerates into a dominant minority, it tries to use force to maintain its undeserved power. The leaders lose touch with their base, and vice versa, and revolution follows.

These words written over fifty years ago describe the situation in France and Belgium in 2005 as the people voted against their proposed European constitution. Is history only repetition? Toynbee answers no, for he believes firmly in the dynamism of the wheel of life, and that civilization is progressive, not recurrent. All the above is the warp and woof of my own philosophy, for a mere repetition in society would bring me, would bring us, to despair. Toynbee believes that all declines are based in the spiritual part of man, which leads Toynbee to his thesis that though it is the outside blows that stimulate, it is the inner ones that destroy the spirit and lead to the breakdown of civilizations.

Failure of Self-DeterminationToynbee says that civilizations break down, or begin to decay and die, from what amounts to suicide. Toynbee lists several reasons why self-determination fails, mostly from short-sighted ideas that undermine creativity.

He quotes Shakespeare's *King John*: "This England never did, nor ever shall/ Lie at the proud foot of a conqueror/But when it first did help to wound itself/… nought shall make us rue/If England to itself do rest but true."

How often have I thought the same, while turning my apartment's triple locks; that I worry about the thief from outside on occasion, but constantly fear the traitor within. And also within me. And how did communism die? From the look of pained surprise on the face of the elder President Bush, you know it wasn't anything he did; no, communism committed suicide, assisted by Gorbachov. As Le Carre's protagonist in *The Secret Pilgrim* said: "It was their emperor, not ours, who had the nerve to mount the rostrum and declare he had no clothes."

I think Toynbee's conclusion that the loss of self-determination results in breakdown is the inverse of his previous conclusion that self-determination is the criterion of growth. Democracy is the political expression of humanitarianism and self-determination. Since humanitarianism and slavery are natural foes, you cannot have one existing with the other. Slavery is inherently evil because it deprives fellow human beings of their essential human dignity, but the Industrial Revolution gave it a new life and a new impetus, especially in the United States.

Lincoln and the Civil War destroyed slavery in the United States just in time to prevent it from destroying both democracy and the fledgling Union. Toynbee's conclusion from this is that war and slavery are anachronistic and fruitless. If we can evolve a leader of our world with the ability to avoid both political and economic nationalism, we have the potential of seeing democracy put its drive into abolishing war as it has abolished slavery.

If our industrial society, or capitalism or market economy is to achieve its potential, it must do so through worldwide cooperation. And that includes those furthest apart, at political and ideological poles.

Failure of Ephemeral Self

Toynbee says that the next error common to society is idolization of an ephemeral self. Toynbee cites Judaism and its concept of monotheism giving rise to an apparently related concept of the Jews as the chosen people. Toynbee equally castigates his favorites, the ancient Greeks, concluding that because they could not create world order in the fifth century BC, they were unteachable.

Toynbee next advocates a position that I consider weak, namely that the Egyptian pharaohs, the pyramid-builders, hastened their civilization's collapse because they spent so much time and treasure on their pyramids. The pyramids and all the other temples, carvings, and statues of that long and glorious era served as a unifying force for their people; in effect, it became their "bread and circuses," without which they may have lacked the unity to support their pharaoh and their civilization.

I admire the Egyptian civilization because it lasted so much longer than any other and was the first to deserve the name of "civilization." To ridicule that civilization because it built pyramids instead of dams or hospitals is to say that today we should turn our museums into homes for the homeless.

Chapter Seven
Disintegration of Civilization

In his fifth volume, Toynbee wrote further about the disintegration of civilization, building on the idea that disintegration happens from within. He explored the nature of disintegration, the schisms in society and individual, and the relationship between the two.

As he mentioned before, Toynbee sees internal discord as the precursor to breakdown, which reverses the process of growth from yin to yang. He says that disintegration is a movement from yang to yin, or from creative growth to satisfaction with the present. The creative minority only leads by "charm." It persuades the majority to mimesis through charisma.

The most obvious example of creative imitation is in a civilization's art. According to Toynbee, most isolated civilizations which produce "art" have had contact, somehow, somewhere, with more advanced civilizations. The more distant the connection, the less impact the major civilization has. A British coin of 100 BC resembles its Macedonian original, but looks a caricature for imitation has become travesty. This theory does not adequately explain Aztec and especially Mayan art, but that may be because we, as members of Western civilization, have not yet discovered the connection.

The sophisticated level of Mayan art suggests to me that one of two things must be true: either the Mayans had a distant connection with a greater civilization, or the Mayan civilization evolved longer than we now know, and evolved this sophisticated culture the same way our Western civilization did in Europe and Asia. The importance of this process of developing a sophisticated culture holds true for a growing civilization; but for a disintegrating civilization this creativity is replaced by force.

Three Forces

Now, Toynbee says that every civilization has three forces acting upon it: political, economic, and cultural, and that these three exert equal force in the process of growth. When growth ceases, the charm or charisma disappears, although the economic and political growth may continue or even accelerate. The cultural element, which is the essence of any civilization, shrivels and turns to force, thereby destroying itself.

The political and economic forces are relatively trivial manifestations of any civilization's existence, and therefore it follows that the most spectacular economic and political triumphs are imperfect and precarious, lacking culture.

Those who follow the path of violence always end in self-inflicted disaster. Only those who follow "a prophet of gentleness" can exert charisma and excite mimesis. When a civilization disintegrates and force and violence become dominant, the people most distant from that civilization become hostile to it, losing their desire for mimesis except in mimicking violence. Soon the influential contact between the civilizations, which had been a zone or area, of mimetic cooperation, becomes a hardened line, a geographical divider between the civilization on one side and barbarians on the other. Toynbee's Law states that this progression is always in favor of the barbarians.

A classic example of this is of two military leaders, Alexander and Napoleon, who failed to learn the above lessons, while a third, Ataturk, learned them and succeeded.

Mustafa Kemal Ataturk, father of Turkey and founder of the nation, had a military education and background. His charisma apparently sprang from his military victories in Gallipoli in World War I, and in Smyrna, present-day Izmir, shortly thereafter. Yet Ataturk was a "prophet of gentleness" who induced mimesis throughout the nation he was creating, a mimesis still active and growing in 2007 both economically and politically, while his country's indigenous culture is both growing and forming the vibrant soul of Turkey.

Ataturk was fortunate in being born when he was, just as Turkey was fortunate in having his genius available in her hour of need. The Ottoman Empire and civilization was near the end of its long disintegration, and it remained to be seen what would happen to the pieces left over at the end of World War I. Greece, Bulgaria, and Syria, to mention just a few of its neighbors, looked hungrily at those bits and pieces and made plans to seize what they could. Ataturk had the intuition to recognize that several things were requisite to survive and to create a new nation, and chief among these was leadership.

Like Alexander and Napoleon before him, Ataturk was the right man at the right time; unlike the other two, Ataturk had the innate wisdom to realize his limits and to design his future within them.

If Alexander had stopped at Persia and consolidated his empire at that time, he might have shone in history as truly great. He lacked this inner wisdom, however, and his existence was more like a runaway train than a carefully designed career with a destination point in view. Alexander lacked a worldview, despite conquering most of the then-known world, and he did not comprehend civilization and its meaning.

Napoleon had a better grasp of the importance of both political and economic forces and their meaning to civilization. Yet, more so than Alexander, Napoleon had an overdose of hubris, the deadly Greek virus that infects us all. His invasion of Egypt was a striking instance of his hubris moving wastefully to destruction.

That his Egyptian campaign ended satisfactorily for him at first is irrelevant to the final moment and meaning of Napoleon's life. Russia was the final moment of madness, or hubris, that displayed Napoleon's weakness for all the world to see. As he pathetically eked out his decline on St. Helena, did Napoleon understand this? Did he think about his life and draw wisdom from his vast and unusual experience?

Nah. Did he leave anything in our history books except evidence of a boorish excess of hubris? Not really, and that's the shame of this gifted fellow, for he could have written a book ranking with the greatest of the nineteenth century if he had tried.

Alexander and Napoleon were two of the world's greatest figures, known to every schoolchild, yet what is their legacy? Did they create a nation? Did they forge a system that outlived them? The answer to both questions is no, and neither Alexander's library nor Napoleon's *Code* counts in the grander scheme of things. If either had created only a great library, or a great code of law, they would have a more secure place in history, in mine at least, for those are real accomplishments with lasting meaning for civilization. Take away from those accomplishments the awful facts of the rest of their lives, lives of essential waste to both their own civilization and to ours, to say nothing of the dreadful waste of life they both committed, and both Alexander and Napoleon come up minuses.

Ataturk, on the other hand, was probably just as great a military genius as either Napoleon or Alexander, but he knew instinctively when to turn away from military violence and clasp peace to his bosom. This is a psychological understanding both Napoleon and Alexander lacked. Ataturk not only left the nation he created with a sense of peace ("Peace at home, Peace in the world"), but he also imbued his people with the concept of non-violence and containment within their geographical borders.

Any modern-day tourist can witness Ataturk's legacy for themselves by visiting Istanbul, but even better is to see the country outside of Istanbul, from the tourist havens on Turkey's west coast to the wonders of the ancients further east, where the people of Turkey demonstrate the lessons that Ataturk bequeathed to them.

Perhaps Western civilization is close to completely eliminating "barbarism" in this millennium; what then? Probably nothing, since civilization's disintegration is always internal, never external—it is always death by suicide. Yet this is irrelevant, for barbarism will always exist; we in our Western civilization make our own. Think of Hitler, Mussolini, and Stalin for a few of the twentieth century's barbarians. These homegrown barbarians are worse than alien ones because they inherited the means to be constructive, but they elected to degenerate into destruction. We each contain the seeds of our own destruction; it is civilization's duty to educate us to keep them under control.

Schism in the Soul, or Self

Toynbee believed that a schism in the individual soul was part of the disintegration of a civilization. This schism within an individual can take several differing paths. A retreat toward archaism, the good old days, the golden days of our forefathers, is one path; others look instead toward a brighter future.

Either one is a failure because the individual is escaping from the microcosm to the macrocosm; in effect, they are fleeing from their own soul because of their fear of necessary spiritual change.

Instead of spiritual change, the individual seeks the same society, or soul, as once existed or might exist in the future, according to Toynbee. My thinking on this is that people who adopt either archaism or futurism end in violence, self-destructive violence. Why? Because they have broken one of the great laws: harmony.

Look at any of the ugly buildings in our cities today—I'm thinking of Athens' rows of apartments. Study these, and you'll discover that their essential ugliness derives from a lack of harmony. Recall my discussion on Andrea Palladio in Chapter One. When you live in a building without harmony, you participate in its lack of harmony and soon your own harmony is at risk. When you lack harmony you are not at peace with yourself, your soul is in schism, and you become unstable and hence prone to violence.

Therefore, a disintegrating civilization begins by losing harmony within itself, evidenced by a culture or art form that lacks harmony. Not just architecture suffers, but painting, sculpture, and especially music demonstrate this lack. Perhaps the twentieth century's atonal music was but a noisy forecast of the violence which has torn the world apart since.

The opposite of discord or schism in the soul is that inner harmony described by Christ: "the Kingdom of God is within you." As a civilization disintegrates there are still flashes of creative growth, even among the mediocre; Toynbee suggests that average teachers may still allow students to catch fire from their unremarkable words. Toynbee writes that Christianity's early success was due in large part to the fact that Christianity alone of the major religions expressed its creed in Greek language and philosophy. Christianity failed to win over China because Rome decreed that its Jesuit missionaries could not express their creed in Chinese terms, as they wished to do.

The Creative Genius as Savior

One of the final elements in this volume of Toynbee's *A Study of History* concerns the relation between disintegrating societies and individuals, in particular a society's various saviors.

In a growing civilization, the creator must play the part of a military leader who meets the challenge with a victory, whereas in a disintegrating civilization he must be a savior who rescues a society which has failed because the situation has turned the creative minority into a non-creative bully.

As part of this section, Toynbee cites examples of why the savior with his sword is foredoomed to failure, concluding that those who live by the sword are doomed to so die.

Next he turns to the detached savior, who usually appears as a philosopher in his detachment, an individual like Adlai Stevenson or Mario Cuomo. He cites Plato in depth and at length, then concludes that the philosopher king is also foredoomed to failure, a conclusion with which I disagree. I consider it frivolous of Toynbee to cite Plato's own experience as proof, and his next argument that the philosopher king's subjects might begin by giving their ruler their support, although eventually the ruler would resort to force, is equally academic.

Surprisingly, he cites Machiavelli as proof that Plato is wrong. What Toynbee misses out on here is personal experience, for only those who, like Machiavelli, have undergone the exigencies of political practice can fully appreciate the problems associated with it. Those real problems, though, can be summed up in two words: human nature. Machiavelli knew full well that every act of a ruler had to be in concord with human nature, or else that ruler would be obliged to make them believe by force.

Toynbee probably did not read all that Machiavelli wrote, and perforce missed the great biography of him published in 1990 (*Machiavelli in Hell* by Sebastian de Grazia), attesting to his understanding. If Toynbee had had some experience outside academia, and even the army in World War I would have been an enlightenment, as he admitted in his final book *Experiences*, he might have understood that a ruler can be smart enough to know human nature and to employ it wisely, and also wise enough to know he can only rule with the consent of the governed.

He neglects to discuss all those rulers who practiced this, from Solomon to Winston Churchill, and especially Ataturk, who succeeded in creating a nation and endowing it with these attributes. Personally, I believe in the role of a philosopher king since most of my life has been lived with that ideal in mind, if not always in fact. I learned my maternal grandfather's precepts early in life, and was able to formulate my own philosophy based upon them, resulting in personal vindication of Plato's and Machiavelli's and my grandfather's judgments.

The post-Toynbee example illustrating my point is the collapse of communism, from 1989 to 1992. As has been clearly documented in newspapers, on TV, and through many books, communism collapsed because it was counter to human nature, not because of economics or denial of God.

Conclusion

Toynbee sums up the first half of his *A Study of History* saying that every civilization meets successive challenges with successful responses until they meet one that they cannot adequately respond to, at which point the society breaks down and begins to disintegrate. The difference between growth and decay is innate in the diversity of growth and the uniformity of disintegration. Yet both contain the same rhythms of yin and yang, challenge and response, which would be meaningless if they went back and forth like a shuttle in a loom. Instead, they weave the story, the History of Man, and it's not dully repetitious but rather a living testimonial to the hope that is inherent in human nature.

Chapter Eight
Religion and the Second Half of
Toynbee's A Study of History

Toynbee writes about universal states and universal churches in his second set of books in this series, but it is in reading his later works, especially *Experiences* and *An Historian's Approach to Religion*, that one really sees how time influences his conclusions.

Toynbee describes many civilizations, but I wonder in how many of them, if any, could he have been educated to the point of being able to write his *Study*? And under how many rulers would he have had the freedom to write what he did? Since Toynbee did become educated in our Western civilization, and wrote under a series of its rulers, to what pressures did he succumb in order to flavor his *Study* so heavily toward Christianity and the early Greek civilization? If he had been a contemporary of Machiavelli's, living in Firenze (Florence) under the Medici, he could have acquired the necessary education, but his "leanings" would have been as different as Machiavelli's were.

For example, Toynbee's first five books in *A Study of History* were written before World War II, during a time of depression and need, whereas the second group of books were written after World War II during a different time and indeed a different space. His ideas about Christian missionaries written after the war reflected the difference, and could not have been written even a few years before the war. His later volume on universal churches would likewise not have been possible during the 1930s, with its claim that man is performing a social act when he seeks God.

This revolutionary idea was not developed by Toynbee in his *Study*, but was dealt with in his last book, *Experiences*, where he was obviously free of all academic or any other restraints from his rulers. In *Experiences*, Toynbee concludes the thought process that he starts above with his humanistic dictum: "God is a human helping another human." Toynbee felt strongly that a religion which wins converts because of its intrinsic merits does not fail when the political regime which exploited it for non-religious purposes fails. Pursuing the social context, Toynbee suggests that man is a social animal, needing continual contact with other humans to develop. Returning to Frazier's *The Golden Bough*, Toynbee asks whether social values and spiritual ones are antithetical. Frazier answers yes, while Toynbee and I say no.

Man is acting socially in searching for God. Toynbee concentrated on this dictum for years, and finally wrote in his book *An Historian's Approach to Religion* that reason is essential to human well-being. Toynbee connected that thought to his summation of the Industrial Revolution of Western civilization, claiming that this was not the entrance to a promised land, but rather to a wasteland. Yet his rationale differs from T. S. Eliot's in that he considered science, with its rule over nature, as less important than man's rule over himself.

Toynbee concludes that if science and religion could cooperate in man's search for inner meaning, it would create an opportunity for the individual to explore his own microcosm successfully. Toynbee's next conclusion, based on the above, is that mankind lives spiritually through his subconscious rather than through his intellect.

This conclusion could have been written by Carl Jung, who lived and wrote contemporaneously with Toynbee, although they were not aware of each other until after World War II, as each of them was developing differing phases of what Jung called the unconscious. Toynbee recapitulates that a growing civilization exhibits harmony among its political, economic, and cultural elements, while a disintegrating civilization exhibits discord among these three primary elements.

The Heroic Age

In addition to the discord in political, economic, and cultural elements present in a disintegrating civilization, when that civilization uses military barriers to hold back the barbarians, the barbarians have time on their side. Eventually, the barbarians will win, although it may take centuries. But when they do win, and eliminate the old dominant civilization, they also remove all military and other restraints. The barbarian civilization then runs amok and enters its "heroic" age, or adolescent age.

Richard Wagner's eponymous hero Siegfried began life with the drawback of having parents who were twins, suggesting a shallow gene pool, and he was a typically ignorant adolescent, called a "hero" because he was too dumb to know fear. Siegfried also exhibited all the other characteristics attributed to a newly free barbarian civilization, just as I did when the U.S. Army liberated me from parental control at the age of seventeen. I didn't recognize it at the time, but I became a "hero," exhibiting all the same characteristics that Siegfried did. It's such an interesting, yet dangerous, way to grow up; for many heroes, like Siegfried, die of their ignorance.

More unfortunately, they tend to take other innocents with them, and then achieve immortality through some poet such as Homer or Wagner. The heroic age a civilization goes through lasts about as long as any adolescence, exhibiting all the idiosyncrasies that Siegfried and I lived through, and then, as Toynbee notes, the surest sign of both its rise and its decline is the epiphany and eclipse of its "heroic" ideals. As these ideals fade, their disappearance evokes a cry of despair. Most doomsayers who live and write about these ages are harrowed by the illusory conviction that the withdrawal of these glimmering lights that have sustained the children of the Dark Age is a portent of the onset of darkness.

Many of these heroes are distinguished by military feats, but they are incapable, being adolescent, of creating institutions. From Agamemnon to Napoleon, including Alexander (whose followers, especially Ptolemy, were the ones who created the institutions), we have examples suggesting that the military mind is not given to the creation of institutions, although the twentieth century has seen such exceptions as de Gaulle, Eisenhower, and Ataturk.

Toynbee goes on to point out that although barbarians make a hash of society, economics, and politics, their bards make good poetry, albeit mainly epic because art favors failure over success. Toynbee realized that the only result achieved by humans who seek to rob their fellows of their humanity is to divest themselves of their own humanity. Or, to repeat the laws of nature and the law of God: natural law is recurrent, like a wheel turning without a wheelwright, turning forever without purpose.

But in reality, all wheels have wheelwrights and drivers and a purpose. Toynbee illustrates this point with Western civilization's war cycles, beginning at the end of the fifteenth century, after the Muslims lost Spain and Columbus found America and financed Spain's expansion. Both events helped Spain launch the Armada in 1588. The next events in this sequence were France at Blenheim, and then Napoleon at Waterloo, and finally Germany in both 1918 and 1945.

Growth takes place whenever a challenge evokes a successful response that, in turn, induces a further and different challenge.

Indeed, as soon as a social breakdown occurs, the tendency toward variety and differentiation that is characteristic of the growth phase is replaced by a tendency toward uniformity. This tendency shows its power by triumphing sooner or later over interference from the outside as well as recalcitrance from within. Toynbee and I agree that the reign of freedom, which thus keeps the laws of nature at bay, is precarious inasmuch as it depends on two exacting conditions. The first is that the conscious personality must keep the subconscious underworld of the psyche under the control of will and reason. The second is that it must also dwell together in unity with the other conscious personalities in this world. These two necessary conditions for freedom are actually inseparable, for when people fall out, the subconscious psyche escapes from the control of each of them.

The hope in all the above is that some different and new chance for society's survival will be discovered that does not use force. Toynbee is obviously hopeful for the future of mankind, and were he alive today he could illustrate the reasons for his hope by citing the current work of the United Nations as well as the death of communism. He might also speculate on Western civilization peacefully becoming a universal state. In other words, time frames of human acceleration or retardation have little to do with natural laws. Toynbee concludes this idea by claiming that the challenge and response of life is always a matter of humanity's freedom of choice.

Chapter Nine
Law and Freedom in History

Toynbee starts his discussion about the relation between law and freedom in history by suggesting that man lives by two laws, one of which is the law of God, which is freedom itself under another name. As has already been established, breakdown or disintegration is in every case a result of a failure of self-determination. In other words, a lack of self-discipline or moral sense in the individual results in breakdown and then disintegration, first in just the individual, but then in the society.

Toynbee thought that the alienation of the internal proletariat was the real sign of the disintegration of society. By the internal proletariat he means those people who feel disaffected by their society or out of touch with it. Surely he would have cited the example of the former Soviet Union losing touch with its own proletariat before it disintegrated.

Prospects of World War III

Toynbee wrote this volume in 1956 and based his thesis mainly on the fact that there were two world powers, the Soviet Union and the United States. Therefore, he made predictions that were valid for 1956, but he could not have anticipated that the Soviet Union would disintegrate in 1990. One of his early conclusions is that in an international balance of power, two is an awkward number. I think he would agree in 2007 that one is even more awkward unless it develops into a universal state.

Along the way, with another world war in mind, he correctly notes that history shows that mutual fear is as potent a source of warlike aggression as is economic want. Since he wrote those words, we've witnessed at least three wars based on mutual fear: the United States in Vietnam, the Soviets in Afghanistan, and the United States in Afghanistan and Iraq.

Toynbee next differentiates between the USSR and the USA, citing the example of their various actions following World War II. The USSR removed all the industrial plants they could from Germany, eastern Europe, and Manchuria and other parts of China they then controlled, leaving these conquered, or "liberated," countries stripped naked. By doing so, they were following historic example, but the United States took the opposite tack through the Marshall Plan, extending large and effective help to all countries, including equally allies and former enemies.

Toynbee wrote about the structure of the United Nations in 1955 and found it wanting, concluding that some other federal structure must be invented to save the world from a third war. If he were writing in 1992 or today in 2006, he would agree that the UN does need restructuring, but it also represents the best hope for the world, and its chance of success remains good, if ephemeral.

After this discussion, he appends a conclusion titled "How This Book Came to be Written." He notes that primitives had never been historically-minded, because their society had always spoken to them not of history, but of nature. Their festivals were not a Fourth of July or Guy Fawkes Day, but rather the unhistorical days of the annually recurrent agricultural year. Therefore, history is a fairly recent matter for mankind, except for the odd Thucydides or other observer of facts.

What intrigues Toynbee and made his *Study* virtually his lifework is his "study" of history and its reasoning behind the bare facts. He was truly fascinated by why civilizations break down and disintegrate, or "what was this Door of Death through which so many once flourishing civilizations had already disappeared?" This is Toynbee's final question. This was his reason for writing this magnificent twelve-volume *A Study of History* over some thirty-five years, and remains mine for studying his *Study* for the past thirteen years. Today, in 2007, the place of honor in my library in Italy is filled with the twelve volumes of *A Study of History*, plus Toynbee's other books and writings, and the library is named for my friend and mentor Dr. Roy P. Fairfield who introduced me to Toynbee's writing.

Chapter Ten
An Historian's Approach to Religion

No discussion that includes Toynbee would be complete without mentioning his book *An Historian's Approach to Religion*.

Toynbee felt strongly about religion, and expressed his feelings about the subject in two lectures that he gave at the University of Edinburgh in 1952 and 1953, from which this book of his is drawn. I won't review this book since a lot of it is also about his *Study*, which I've written about above, but I'll comment on the part of his attitude toward religion that he did not touch on in his *Study*.

Toynbee wrote that universal knowledge needed to be turned into ideas that would affect the masses. I reply to this by saying that myth is the means to make the permanent temporarily accessible. Furthermore, opera, or also music or poetry, is a means to make myth more accessible. But Toynbee was speaking of religion as another branch of myth, and I strongly suspect that he thought so, although he was put in a straightjacket by convention, as I've remarked above.

I think that Toynbee was trying to wheedle his way out of a dilemma of his own making. He wanted to be honest, but he was enmeshed by his own net, the words he had written and lectured on for almost four decades. This is the same dilemma that most of us suffer from, known as growing old or, as I would put it, maturing. Toynbee was approaching the time when he could speak frankly about religion, but he was not quite there, and he was writing his way completely around the subject, looking for the exit.

I've done the same, and I respect his intellectual confusion almost as much as I admire his conclusions. Furthermore, Toynbee writes that acts of worship, from the richest pageant of a pope saying a pontifical mass at St. Peter's to the simple, yet equally moving scene of masses of Muslims kneeling and praying to the same

God five times a day, tend to become institutionalized when the congregation extends beyond the family circle.

Yet Toynbee says that God can be worshipped individually as well as congregationally, in any place at any time, with or without formalities, for God is a spirit; as I have cited frequently, Toynbee defines God as one human helping another. Toynbee felt strongly that shrines, rituals, and social conventions may be highly charged with feeling, yet myth is a far more potent force at the heart of religion.

Toynbee writes that sacrificing, or throwing out, the non-essentials is painful, especially to religious individuals and intellectuals; but the most painful thing of all is losing self-centeredness. If we don't search out the mystery of the universe through curiosity, suffering will bring it to us.

We can see the universe from differing angles, and from each angle it is different. From one angle it appears spiritual, while from another it appears physical, and from each of these it wears a different aspect. Toynbee claims that human nature is a union of opposites that are not only incongruous but contrary and conflicting; the conflicting elements are not only united in nature, they are inseparable from each other, which brings us full circle to Toynbee's dictum: Deus est mortale iuvare mortalem, or God is one human helping another.

Toynbee's *A Study of History*, in its place of honor in my library, is, as I have said, one of the most influential set of books I've ever read. It is especially interesting to compare it to his *Experiences,* which was written later.

Section Three:
Creative Mythology

o o o o o o o o o o o o o o o o o o o o o o o o o o o o o o o o o o

Facts of the mind made manifest in a fiction of matter.

—Maya Deren, philosopher and aunt to Genji Ito,
an actor and musician with whom
I often worked,
who gave me this quote.

Chapter Eleven
Religion and Myth

Arnold Toynbee wrote feelingly about religion, and considered there to be a link between religion and myth, but he never fully explained this relationship. I believe, as anyone who studies the earlier civilizations of the Fertile Crescent must, that the two are inextricably linked.

As in the first two sections of this book, in this section I'll follow in the tracks of a single author, Joseph Campbell, through at least three of his books. Also, as with Gibran and Toynbee in the first two sections, I'll use others writers both extensively and intensively. In particular, I'll reference Carl G. Jung and his specific writings on mythology, with cross-references from mythological sources such as Bulfinch, Robert Graves, Edith Hamilton, Mary Renault, and Homer.

Early Religions

The earlier religions, as opposed to the earliest, were about love and war; the Babylonians' Ishtar was the double goddess of both love and war, just as the later Aphrodite/Venus of the Greek and Roman pantheon was linked closely with their god of war, Ares/Mars. With thousands of years of virgin births related in those earliest myths, was it any wonder that Christ was proclaimed as such? Or that Mary was received so joyously in the very area where Aphrodite ruled?

I can understand why Islam treats Mary as a queen and one of the greatest women in the Koran, for she was the mother of a prophet of Islam (Christ). Yet she is not considered divine by Islam, which creates an anomalous situation for Christianity as well as for those seeking closer ties between mythology and religion.

I am a big fan of the *Epic of Gilgamesh*, and in 1993 I bought the long-awaited *La Saga di Gilgamesh* in Italian, translated by Giovanni Pettinato, an Assyriologist at L'Universita La Sapienza di Roma. He translated the cuneiform tablets from the Hittite capital, Hattusas, in eastern Turkey, matching that story with the previously known ones. Pettinato also gives an index of the gods in the Hittite days, roughly the second millennium before Christ.

A fascinating example from his book that I did not know before is that of Alallu, who is described in full as a "mythical bird, one of the unfortunate lovers of Ishtar according to the classic epic." The description of Ishtar herself is interesting for it lends insight into her relationships: "The Babylonian name of the goddess of love and of war (see Inanna). Daughter of An, or, according to other traditions, of Sin. Sister of Ereshkigal and of Shamash, and a multiple goddess of Uruk." These quotes are from Dr. Pettinato's translation of *The Saga of Gilgamish*.

Uruk is where Gilgamesh ruled, located in present-day southern Iraq. It gets both interesting and complex as we look up the references in Ishtar's biography as written by Pettinato. Inanna is the "Sumerian goddess of love, war, and regality." Like Ishtar, she is a multiple goddess of Gilgamesh's city, Uruk, as well as a daughter of An. It sounds very much as though they are the same goddess with different names. An himself is no less than the Sumerian god of heaven, the father of the gods, the head of the pantheon, and one of Uruk's multiple gods, who co-divides the temple Eanna with Inanna and Ishtar. He sounds like a combination of the later Cronos and his son Zeus.

Sin, Ishtar's other putative father, is one of Ur's gods, the god of the moon. Sin was on a par with Shamash, Ishtar's brother, the god of the sun; Shamash ruled during the day while Sin ruled at night. Those last four words sound strangely in English, eh? There's no need here to get involved with the rather academic differences between these texts and the others; let it be enough to say everyone should read the *Epic of Gilgamesh*, for it's our earliest bible, our first written myth, and important to all that follows, especially the Testaments and the Koran.

Chapter Twelve
Joseph Campbell

Now, how to start a discussion on mythology, or one on religion-mythology? From a lifetime of immersion in mythology, first as "fairy" stories, then as religion, then as a fascination with the Greek gods and the Trojan War, culminating in studying mythology as a vital element in society and a major contributing element in civilization, I have become mesmerized by the repetition of mythological elements throughout history, as evidenced by the opening description of Ishtar.

As a start, however, I prefer to leave the gods to themselves and work with Joseph Campbell and his writings, though I will also show how closely Jung's thoughts are related. One regret I have is that I missed a seminar Campbell gave years ago. I compounded that error by never even attending one of his lectures. I have partially atoned for the error by reading all of his books. Throughout his books called collectively *The Masks of God*, Campbell stresses that we need myths to steer our lives by.

My own life has given me an opportunity to apply this principle. I lived through the end of communism, staying in each of the six countries of Eastern Europe, and then in the Soviet Union. Recalling my anthropological training as well as my life in journalism, I was deeply interested in the bewilderment of these peoples whose central myth was suddenly declared bankrupt. Worse, the villain was declared alive and well, while their own hero was dead. It was like discovering that the God you'd been raised on and believed in all your life, did not exist, and communism was the Truth!

In 1992, I saw daily evidence of this disturbing psychological and religious event, from former communists marching in Moscow to demonstrate their loyalty to their "god," to the people of Yugoslavia turning their backs to ancient enmities in order to justify their existence. A partial answer to this worldview upheaval is to substitute other myths for those destroyed, which the various Christian churches have tried, mainly successfully, to do in Eastern Europe and Russia. This is also what Turkey is doing for the Moslem and Turkic-speaking former republics of the Soviet Union.

Campbell uses the Renaissance to illustrate the power of myth in a society, citing the example of when the flat-earth theories were being challenged by the first stirrings of Western science. Small wonder that the Catholic Church was scared into starting their Inquisition. Without those myths, apparently derived from the Bible and hence the word of God, the medieval Church thought that it would cease to exist.

Campbell speculates on what might have been accomplished if the Church and civilization had adopted a more tolerant view toward these new theories, but I think that here he misses one of the points of history, which is why I spent so much time in section two of this book. Civilization, per se, needs intolerance and persecution to stay alive, even when the world seems headed for chaos. As Toynbee explained, the apparent end of the world is usually just the arrival of a creative phase that heralds the true miracles of man, such as interplanetary travel and exploration of the inner workings of the mind.

Campbell writes that with the loss of a myth there follows uncertainty, since life requires life-supporting illusions. When these are gone, there is nothing secure to hold onto; no moral law, nothing firm. Campbell asks, "since our cherished myths have been demolished by science, what substitute shall we use to keep our civilization from disintegrating in a wave of lawlessness, vice, and disease? Should the teacher be loyal first to the supporting myths of our civilization or to the 'factualized' truths of his science?"

He concludes that psychology will provide the answer, especially when it studies the source and nature of myth. Many of our most-cherished myths will be proven "false" along the way, or, as the quote at the beginning of this chapter suggests, myths will become "facts of the mind made manifest in a fiction of matter." Campbell adds that we must not only deal with "facts of the mind," but also evolve techniques for retaining them. I prefer Toynbee's description, which I explained in Chapter Two above, where he spells out the need for both a macrocosmic view as well as the inner microcosmic one. Campbell goes on to quote from many, such as Freud, who would merely destroy the myth without understanding the need to replace it. This all changed with Carl Jung, of course, who viewed mythology and religion as positive forces in life.

Jung concludes that what is needed is a dialogue between adherents of myth and proponents of scientific theory, not a fixture at either pole: a dialogue by way of symbolic mythology. Giordano Bruno was burned at the stake in Rome in 1600 for professing that the earth went around the sun. Bruno declared that dissension is dangerous, and therefore authoritative doctrine is needed, and this declaration was dangerous for him at that time because he added that the Church had no right to interfere with the pursuit of knowledge.

Elks, Masons, and Rotarians amass their own language in an attempt to achieve their own mythological place in life. The more they succeed, the more powerful and enduring their zone is. Campbell continues to show that Dante's great works were not just inspired by Islam and Muslim writers, but Dante copied them, sometimes verbatim, without attribution. This is an unfortunate but common footnote in history, as we shall explore next.

Chapter Thirteen
Role of Islam

After Muhammad's followers were territorially successful, Baghdad became the center of the world for five hundred years, from AD 750 to 1258. As Western civilization entered its "dark" years, Islam flourished. The really curious aspect of this is that 99 percent of Western students know nothing of Islam and its immense significance and contribution to Western civilization.

Western history books have very little information about Islam, leaving a blank that is reminiscent of the former Soviet Union's "selective" history. Why aren't Western civilization's students taught this? But there's more to it than this: consider the Christian Crusades, for instance. The religious fervor whipped up by Western civilization in support of those Crusades obscured any similarities between Islam and Christianity, probably intentionally.

When I was an undergraduate student at Princeton University, I was considered at least "unusual" for spending a whole year with Professor Philip K. Hitti in the study of Islamic culture. And Princeton was, and is, one of the very few Western universities to give any space or time to Islam.

It isn't products of one civilization that influence another, but rather the creators within the emerging civilization who "absorb" the ideas from the other civilization. Toynbee would say that it's the growing civilization's dominant minority who are creators, and they absorb the ideas of a disintegrating civilization and put them into effect in a new way. In effect, they re-create the foreign idea. Without this charismatic group within a growing civilization, the foreign idea would not germinate, largely because the majority has nobody to follow.

An even more basic law of mine is that the mature ideas created in one place which catalyze the mass of pubescent ideas in another place are vital to that emerging culture. Therefore, Islamic culture was essential to Western civilization during its Renaissance in the thirteenth and fourteenth centuries, even though it is largely unacknowledged.

Averroes (1126–98) goes further, classifying people into three categories or levels of understanding. Since the two lesser categories comprise most of mankind, he avers that the Koran's images and likenesses were designed by God to summon these lesser intellects "to assent to those images, since it is possible for assent to those images to come about through the indications common to all men, i.e., the dialectical and rhetorical indications. This is the reason why scripture is divided into apparent and inner meanings: the apparent meaning consists of those images which are coined to stand for those ideas, while the inner meaning is those ideas themselves, which are clear only to the demonstrative class." These quotes of Averroes are from Campbell's *Oriental Mythology.*

That statement reads very much as if Averroes was a follower of Plato, who wrote about this idea some 1,500 years before. The later Christian St. Thomas Aquinas knew Averroes' writings and came to the same conclusions, thereby transducing Averroes' Islamic philosophy into Western civilization's Christian philosophy, albeit without attribution. Well, not exactly, for in his earlier work, St. Thomas explicitly declares that he copied directly from Maimonides, a follower of Averroes.

Carrying the idea of inner meanings a step further, an oxymoron is necessary to free the mind to perceive the real meaning hidden in myth. An oxymoron also illustrates a human relationship: a lover thinks his woman is a wise virgin, and loves her for both of these qualities, whereas she may be a foolish whore, which is why love is blind.

There is a parallel between religions in their symbols, and Campbell gives an interesting comparison: the Indian god Shiva is similar to the Greek god Poseidon, each with their trident; in Christianity, Shiva/Poseidon becomes the devil, Satan, still with a trident. And then Campbell strikes home for me as he describes Tristan and Isolde, both the story or myth and Richard Wagner's opera. It's one of the stronger operatic stories, mixing stoicism with love, heroes and heroines, reflecting Wagner's personal pain at the time he was composing this opera, and finally reaching for death itself as the solution.

I disagree with Wagner's conclusions that only through death can true love be either realized or fulfilled, but I agree with Nietzsche that Wagner "creates most successfully out of the deepest depths of human delight, as it were from its already emptied chalice, where the bitterest, most unappetising drops have run together with the sweet, for good and for ill," as he wrote in his book *The Birth of Tragedy and The Case of Wagner.*

Thomas Mann suggested in his youthful work, *Tristan*, that Tristan represented Cornish tin, and Isolde Irish copper, a thought that I had never heard before. Perhaps it wasn't so much a love story as a chemical one: the love potion fused their copper and tin into a different kind of bronze age.

The Waste Land

Campbell next asks himself what the "Waste Land" is, and answers that it's where the priests are more powerful than the poets, thereby prefiguring U.S. society in 2006. Campbell, writing some fifty years ago, had words of hope for us in 2006: namely about the emergence of a prophet, a visionary, or a shaman, a person whose insights would lead society to myth to save them from the force of fundamentalism.

Campbell quotes his contemporary, Professor Schaeder, who asserts that power is governed by greed for more than one's share. He adds that the best antidote to greed is love, or self-confidence in the power of love, suggesting that our conception of God as love is the real answer to power gone wrong. I had never heard of Professor Schaeder before reading him being quoted in Campbell's book, but he was a contemporary of Toynbee's, and from his studies of the Orient he deduced the above ideas, remarkably close to Toynbee's ideas but developed from such a different area.

Campbell concludes that our current sense of a "Waste Land" is caused by our knowledge that the Biblical myth of creation is not historically true. Absorbing this knowledge into our societal psyche leads us to believe that there is no participation in divinity on our part, leading to alienation.

Alienation, I would add, only from historical myth, or a fact of the mind made manifest in a fiction of myth. Alienation is evident in our civilization in 2006 through acts of terrorism; the recent bombs in London have revealed it more starkly than most terror acts because the country was better prepared to act than, for example, either the United States or Spain were, including on a journalistic front.

I get the *Times* of London in Italy a day late, but I am impressed by the timeliness of some of their reporting. For example, the day after the bombs in the Underground, the *Times* asked some interesting world leaders for their reaction, including the Chief Rabbi in London, Sir Jonathan Sacks, who commented about what acts of terrorism represent: "It is not the weapon of the weak against the strong, but the rage of the angry against the defenceless and innocent. It is an evil means to an evil end." Also, in the Italian-language *La Repubblica*, which I also read daily, a headline read "Who Can Kill a Daughter of Islam?," referring to a Muslim woman killed by one of the bombs. Yet the most interesting piece of writing about this incident was a London *Times* interview with four Muslims in their late teens in their own neighborhood, near one of the explosion sites. The interviewer was a white Englishman, and as his interviewees condemned the bombings two of their cell phones rang from somewhere within sight; the caller told the Muslim youths to leave, and they quickly did.

The rest of the article confirmed the ambiguous reactions of the local Muslim people. Perhaps they were afraid that they might be blamed for the bombing, but their true feelings were at best amorphous, and thus open to competing interpretations.

Another Italian comment, from politician and philosopher Emma Bonino, was printed in *La Repubblica* in the days following the 2005 London bombings: "I have learned that the difference between us and them is not religion, nor lifestyle or aspirations, but the political system: here there is democracy and there is dictatorship. Nothing else." She sounds like a paraphrase of Campbell's description of the Waste Land, above.

This is the reason I'm writing this book: to show the importance of the great writers of our times to our own thinking and rationalizing of the irrational acts in our lives.

Campbell next quotes Heloise's Abelard, saying that we should read what the Church writes about religion, but with the freedom to judge and decide for ourselves. Heloise had herself a first-class thinker, which unfortunately his Church could not afford at that time. Campbell suggested that Abelard was the Tristan of his day and fought against the Waste Land of his day.

Campbell then mentions one of my favorite authors in this context, Dr. Viktor Frankl, and his great book, *Man's Search for Meaning*. I would add to the above a sense of humor, for I've found time and again that this was the essential element, more so than courage or will, to survive through a desperate time.

I heard Elie Wiesel speak to this point at a journalists' meeting in Venice in 1992, with his poet's voice rising and descending like music as he moved our audience of hardened journalists to a standing ovation.

I'm reminded, also, of a month I spent with Herbie, a Czech survivor of five years in Auschwitz, as we sailed the Turkish coast some twenty-five years ago, and he told me how many of his friends died in that awful place after losing their humor first, and then their will.

Campbell mentions two of my favorite myths in this context, those of Sisyphus and Oedipus. Sisyphus, by rolling his eternal stone uphill each day, symbolizes man's useless labor, but he achieves freedom daily as he follows his stone back to the valley. And this freedom represents his consciousness. Oedipus' trials were different yet similar in scope, and his freedom came at the end of his life as, blind and aged, his daughter Antigone held his hand and he observed that "in spite of all these trials, my advanced age and the grandeur of my soul lead me to conclude that all is well." The quote is from Sophocles' play *Antigone*.

Campbell now mentions Frankel again, who wrote that man is required to bear his inability to rationally understand his significance. Oedipus, self-blinded, is a maimed king, a lame smith, for whom there is no cure. Yet Oedipus, like Camus' Sisyphus, experienced his maimed life and was blessed with the realization that all is well. Yeats is right: sometimes it's better to be blessed with your afflictions rather than being cured of them.

It is fascinating the way in which culminating phrases of great thoughts resonate through our lives. The myth of Sisyphus has resonated in mine for over half a century, and is so much with me I have incorporated a part of it in my daily summer life as I water my Italian garden at sunset, the same time of day when Sisyphus is unchained from his rock and walks downhill in freedom. The steps from one garden to another at my home are one meter from one small riser to the next, allowing me to take one huge step for each, exulting in the completion of one job and feeling as free as Sisyphus, "my shadow at evening striding behind me." The last quote, above, is my paraphrase of T. S. Eliot's lines 28 and 29 from his *Waste Land*.

Campbell, retelling the story of the Grail and other Arthurian myths, describes Parsifal's rejection of Guernamanz's gift of his daughter as a demonstration of his inner knowledge that what is worthwhile in life must be earned from within; it cannot be received as a gift. Campbell suggests that each "Lady of Destiny," or the one woman who resonates in a man's life as Thomas Mann put it, is literally an invitation to death, and each is like the initiate who guides the neophyte to a knowledge beyond death in the Eleusinian Mysteries.

Chapter Fourteen
The Mask of God

The Death of "God"

Erasmus, in his book *In Praise of Folly*, summed up his feelings by describing the Christian religion as folly without wisdom. I discussed aspects of this topic in detail in the previous chapter, but I'll add some thoughts here. I was happy to discover that both Toynbee and I had reached the same conclusion about God early on. We both rejected the possibility that Christ was the son of God, he at age seven and I when I was ten years older. The important thing is that neither of us would have rejected this concept if we had been born five hundred years before. The grasp of the Church on human minds was so inhumanly tight, and the fear of questioning that authority so pervasive, that I believe most would-be dissenters simply blanked such heretical thoughts from their minds, effectively killing the nascent chain of thought, still-born, that could lead to a truly independent concept.

When I sit in my home in Italy's Apennine Mountains, I am filled with wonder that I am here, looking at these storied peaks and valleys, laden with castles and fortresses from yesteryear, where both Caesar and Hannibal trod. I know that many others have sat exactly where I am, and perhaps also wondered at the majesty of it all, especially at sunrise and sunset. Yet the fact that I am unique, uniquely myself just as each of us is, apart from all the others who have sat here or will sit here, and that my uniqueness derives from being here, now, in this effervescent moment, knowing that I shall soon die while these mountains will go on and on, cries out for meaning. Why? Why am I here? What is the meaning? I am eternal in the sense that my feelings are eternal, as is this landscape. Therefore, my participation in this scene, right now, is the meaning, as it was and as it will be, and my being here is the eternal being, and I am the world because I share it, though only for now.

Campbell sums up this thought process of mine in his "Death of God" chapter: "Who is to talk to you or to me of the being or non-being of God unless, by implication, to point beyond his words and himself and all he knows or can tell?"

I have two answers to Campbell's question. The first is that both Toynbee and I define God differently than Campbell does; our definition is also our second answer: Deus est mortale iuvare mortalem, or God is a human helping another human. Campbell concludes his discussion on the death of God with a thought from Nietzsche: morality becomes more necessary as we are freer of theology.

Once again, we have seen and are seeing this principle at work as the former Soviet Union crumbled from within, their old mythology dead and proven wrong, with no other myths to replace it. Anarchy, both within the state and deriving from within each soul, is rampant, giving rise to terrorism. Our obligation is clear: we must supply civilization with new myths to live by. Morality is needed to keep our civilization from being driven apart by the terrorists in our midst.

The Earthly Paradise

My parents and family were dogmatic Roman Catholics, the most narrow-minded sort that God never made. At the age of seventeen I enlisted in the U.S. Army (this was during World War II), and escaped from both parental bonds and religious chains. Yet the training, the memory of rites and guilt, remained. My society was left behind as I sailed on a troopship to Europe, yet I also carried my society with me: unknown, unseen, yet lurking in my soul ready to ambush me whenever I came close to realizing that I wasn't just rejecting society or parents or dogma such as the divinity of Christ, but that I was trying to see that the basis for society was wrong.

I was stumbling toward the idea that society (church, parents, whatever) was not the substance through which I could achieve meaning. No, this concept of my parents, my church, and my society was wrong; for, as Campbell wrote, the truth is the other way round. Yet, beginning from that painfully joyful experience, it required a lifetime of reading, talking, writing, and thinking to appreciate Jung's thought that myth reveals the divine in us.

I think that this is what Campbell means by the "Mask of God" in his book of that title; that is, each of us is a mask of God, just as each of us masks God within ourselves. Campbell quotes one of Wittgenstein's propositions about life meaning not infinity but timelessness, suggesting that eternal life is now. This is something that I have learned to believe in, rather than something that I feel to be true. In order to accept this idea we must let our past loose; as Christ suggested, we must die to the world.

Chapter Fifteen
Occidental Mythology

Joseph Campbell begins this encyclopedic book, volume three in the *Mask of God* series, with some fascinating myths from the Bible; it's especially exciting to compare them to Jung's and Kerenyi's essays on Demeter-Persephone and the Eleusinian Mysteries.

First is Adam and Eve, and Campbell takes the following words from Genesis: "In the sweat of your face, you shall eat bread till you return to the ground; for out of it you were taken; you are dust, and to dust you shall return."

But this dust Campbell that alludes to is Mother Earth, and human beings were not only born of earth, but were to return there upon death, rather than to the father, Yahweh, who had given Adam and Eve life itself.

Campbell builds on the idea that culture flowed from west to east and then from east to west, forming a whole throughout North Africa, Europe, and the Levant. He echoes more precisely what Toynbee said about the origins of Western individualism as opposed to the Eastern philosophy of individual sublimation to the group, or society.

I participated in a modern-day version of this conflict during the five years I lived in Turkey, married to a neolithic Turk and living in a very neolithic, or group, society. I felt the conflict between my individualism and their group concept, and thinking about it helped me to define my own individualism. If anything, the fall of the Berlin Wall in November, 1989, sharpened my sense of individuality, for traveling through the eastern European countries made me wonder in a different way about communism.

My previous thoughts about communism had mainly been formed by writers such as Arthur Koestler and George Kennan; then I had my thinking rearranged at university by writers from a differing background and mental structure than those two giants, namely Sartre and Camus, who were more intellectually attractive to me then than Kennan and Koestler.

My Experience with the East–West Divide

I had a weird influence enter my intellectual life simply because I had learned to speak French in the U.S. Army. In their infinite wisdom, the army sent me to Paris to live for eighteen months at the end of World War II, and I leaped into that environment, including the language (via Berlitz). When I returned to college in the United States, I naturally signed up for a French language course, and was jumped into conversational French where, because my university was small but attractive, Jacques Mauretain was in residence. He was one of the great French intellectuals of the day, and he sat in and talked to us students, even asking my opinion about life in Paris, and so I accepted many of his ideas simply because I was smitten with his charisma.

All the above helped me form my mind about who I was and where I came from, and I exhibited my changing persona in various ways, just as we all do. As I became more and more interested in the difference between East and West, I met a young (thirty-four-year-old) Turkish woman and we began talking sessions, largely because she was a lawyer and I hired her firm to represent me. During the interminable waiting periods we shared in various courts, I plumbed her thoughts about East versus West, and found that her seven years at schools in England had definitely formed her mind as a Westerner, or individualist. Here, at age thirty-four, she was married to a Turk of Eastern thinking and had three small children. I asked the inevitable question as to which side of the East–West divide she was on, and where did her husband stand.

She had obviously thought about this matter far more than I had at her age, and she stated definitively that she was a Westerner and her husband was equally determined to be an Easterner. But, she added, she was instructing her three children to look to the West for their intellectual heritage.

The next question I had was "is it only those Turks who have studied or lived in the West who think of themselves as belonging to the West instead of the East?: No, not necessarily, for my closest Turkish colleague was Hussain, who studied for many years in England, and whose mother was an English woman married to his Turkish father. I helped Hussain change his life from a building contractor to a theater director and actor, and together we produced some interesting theater in New York City as well as in Italy and also Turkey. Hussain struggled for many years, especially while I knew him, between his Western education and leanings, and his Eastern soul. I think that when he tragically died at the age of forty-five, he was at ease intellectually between the two. It's difficult to generalize about the lives of all my friends in Turkey and the Middle East, for each one is an individual life, individually formed by the ideas they encountered and thought through.

Yet the difference between East and West is readily apparent in each of their lives, then as it is today, and somewhere among my friends there is a potential answer to the present question about the meaning of this East–West pendulum in its present swing toward terrorism. The present-day 2005 shock of London bombings being perpetrated by Easterners raised in a Western culture needs investigation and understanding before we Westerners can begin to resolve this problem. I know some of the questions to ask and some of the directions to take, but I have no answers to the sorrows these misguided youths brought to their nation, England, and to their shocked families, and the studied thoughtlessness and insult they gave to their professed religion, Islam.

Chapter Sixteen
Mythic Parallels and Religion

Ianannu and Ishtar

In the second chapter of *Occidental Mythology*, Campbell establishes a link between Ianannu and Ishtar of the earliest Sumerian mythology and the Demeter-Persephone unity explored at length in Jung and Kerenyi's essays on mythology that are reported on in detail later in this book. In later discoveries and writings, Ianannu is found to be even more significant than Campbell imagined, for she is not just a multiple goddess but was also known by another name, Ishtar, daughter(s) of An (analogous to Zeus) and also of Sin, the god of the moon and co-equal with Shamash (Apollo), god of the sun. If the earlier Sumerian mythology has the concept of not just multiple gods and goddesses, but that of a unity, such as we explored regarding Demeter-Persephone, then we have found another link between cultures of differing times and places. Or we have found an apparent anachronism creating a link through anamorphosis.

As the earlier matriarchal system was supplanted by a patriarchal system, the religious system of the former was likewise replaced. In Campbell's words, "All religions contain myths related as facts, posing questions to which answers reflect the mind of the answerer rather than of God." This quote is from the second chapter of *Occidental Mythology*.

Gods and Heroes of the West, 1500–500 BC

Nietzsche was the first to recognize that within Greek heritage there was an interplay of two mythologies: the pre-Homeric Bronze Age heritage of the peasantry, in which release from the yoke of individuality was achieved through group rites inducing rapture, and the Olympian mythology of measure and humanistic self-knowledge that is epitomized for us in Classical art. The glory of the Greek tragic view lay in its recognition of the mutuality of these two orders of spirituality, neither of which alone offers more than a partial experience of human worth. This quote is from Nietzsche's *Zarathustra*.

In chapter four of *Occidental Mythology*, Campbell says that Homer's Troy was in fact just as mighty a city as he described in the *Iliad*, wealthy and with flourishing trade circa 1300–1184 BC, as was contemporary Palestine. Around this time, the Hebrews suddenly erupted into Palestine, the Dorians into Greece, and the Gasga into the Hittite Empire. Was this coincidence? Campbell answers my question, claiming that it is too neat for coincidence, and adds the further question of why in the case of Greece what appeared was poetry, and of the Jews, religion. He does not mention that both of these took centuries to develop, whereas the Hittites seem to have disappeared quickly, perhaps owing to an absence of records.

After Homer's Epics, the Reality of the Polis

In the third section of the book, Campbell relates how the fifth century BC Greeks, having repulsed the Persians four times, were prepared to elevate man's thinking to new heights. Campbell writes that Alexander was Europe's answer to the Persians' defeat and the rise of Greek philosophy and literature, citing as example the fact that Alexander was celebrated as a god within two generations of his death, and was the creator of a new world.

Campbell's assessment of Alexander might be acceptable since he is thinking mainly of Alexander's influence on myth, but I find it strange even in that context. These things happened as a result of Alexander's passing through those parts of the world, not as an occurrence planned by Alexander, which it might have been had Aristotle continued with Alexander and acted upon him as mentor.

Great Rome: 500 BC to AD 500

The Celts preceded the Romans in Europe, penetrating as far as Asia Minor (still called Galatia, hence Istanbul's district of Galatasaray). And they brought with them the forge and the sword, giving power to the shamans who share their love of fire.

Campbell describes the Etruscan part of Italy at length, although he had only read about this area and visited it a few times. I have lived here for over twenty-five years, and simply because of the propinquity have come to feel a kinship, much as Americans living in former Indian places come to develop a kinship with the Indians.

When visitors mention an interest in the Etruscans, I usually tax their interest by reading them Macauley's long poem "Horatio at the Bridge." If they survive that, I take them to Tarquinia, ancient Etruscan capital, and either fire their interest permanently or terminally bore them, but in either case they never forget the Etruscans.

Campbell quotes Dr. von Vacano on the idea that the core of both Celtic Iron Age practices and Etruscan ones was the belief in the transforming power of fire. Such conceptions have found expression in countless tales and legends of smiths, such as the one of the little man who was burned till he became young. These smiths are as lame as Hephaistos, just as poets and seers are often blind, indicating that a heightened ability in one field requires a loss in another, just as Wotan needed to hang, Christ-like, on the world ash tree and lose one outward-seeing eye in order to gain insight. This all suggests that we must all lose something (our youth, perhaps?) to achieve self-knowledge and wisdom.

And perhaps Seneca said it best of all for mankind and his abiding myths as Campbell quotes him from his *Epistles*: "When you find yourself within a grove of exceptionally tall, old trees, whose interlocking boughs mysteriously shut out the view of the sky, the great height of the forest and the secrecy of the place together with a sense of awe before the dense, impenetrable shades will awaken in you the belief in a god. And when a grotto has been hewn into the hollowed rock of a mountain, not by human hands, but by the powers of nature, and to great depth, it pervades your soul with an awesome sense of the religious. We honor the sources of great rivers. Altars are raised where the sudden freshet of a stream breaks from below the ground. Hot springs of steaming water inspire veneration. And many a pond has been sanctified because of its hidden situation or immeasurable depth."

The above are strangely moving words to me, for I have lived for almost a quarter century in a part of Italy where sacred springs and dense woods are a part of daily life. My wife and I were married near Spoleto in a monastery occupied by Saint Francis in 1216, but founded hundreds of years earlier by Benedictines. However, they chose that site because it is in a dense woods such as Seneca describes, and it had already been sacred to locals over two thousand years ago. A stone describing the penalty for desecrating the area is still readable, and many locals today feel as though they can actually physically feel the presence of holy spirits there.

Other numina, according to Campbell, of more constant presence, acquired more substantial character. Consider Jupiter, for instance, lord of the brilliant heavens and of storm, later identified with Zeus; Mars, the war god, equated with Ares; Neptune, the god of waters, identified with Poseidon; Faunus, the patron of animal life, originated as the Greek Silvanus, god of the woods. Comparably, of the female forces, Ceres became identified with Demeter; Telus Mater with Gaia; Venus, originally a Roman market goddess, was identified with the older Aphrodite; and Fortuna with Moira. This list is not exhaustive; there were many others as well.

Mythic Parallels and Religion, Occidental Mythology

Campbell does not examine all the previous virgin births in this chapter, as both he and I have discussed them separately elsewhere, but the acceptance of the concept was present throughout the known world at that time and had been for hundreds of years. Hence the ready acceptance of Mary, the new Aphrodite, or Ishtar, or earth mother, or Demeter-Persephone, or any of the dozens of other names she had had before.

Campbell next suggests that the divine aura, including the Star of Bethlehem, was symbolized by the halo, which first came from Persian art but then travelled east to Buddhist art as well as west to Christian art. History may have lost the track of this traveling process, but the importance derives from the sense of myth and not the factual history therein. Campbell writes at length upon Christ's life and apparent miracles, not as history, but because of the impact they had on history. As he says, Christ was not the first, nor the last, prophet with charismatic power who could work miracles. He mentions some of his predecessors and followers from the Buddha to my favorite, Muhammad.

In the last one hundred pages of *Occidental Mythology*, Campbell examines the interplay of the two great spiritual worlds of the Levantine and European souls, much as Toynbee did a few years before him, arriving at the same conclusion: Islam spread not just the word of God, but encouraged scholars to think and to invent and to write in such a splendid way that it finally flowered in Europe as the Renaissance.

Campbell said in the last pages of *Occidental Mythology* that Islam was a continuation of the Zoroastrian-Jewish-Christian heritage "carried to its ultimate formulation." Even a casual reading of the Koran reveals these roots explicitly, including the description of Abraham as the father of Islam and Jesus Christ as a prophet of Islam, with His mother, Mary, as the second most blessed of women in Islam. Campbell does not elaborate on these "certain portions," but they show Islam, and Muhammad, at their best and most thoughtful.

Just as Christianity today is rife with self-styled prophets who distort and over-look Christ's basic theme of love, so, too, is Islam today choking on its self-styled ayatollahs who forget Muhammad's basic teaching. We are all blood brothers as well as spiritual brothers, and who can hate and fight more fiercely than those? The American Civil War is our own national reminder.

Mary, the mother of Christ, not only had glorious predecessors stretching back millennia to the first Levantine earth mother, but she also had followers, none of whom were more devoted than Moslems. Muhammad and the Koran place her high in their pantheon, in a fashion similar to Christianity except that, like me, they deny her divinity. In Islam, Mary is second only to the divine Fatimah.

There are two aspects of Islam that Joseph Campbell stresses which illustrate the basic difference between East and West, society versus the individual. First is the shamanistic way. As Omar Khayyam illustrated the concept in his *Rubaiyat*: "Man is a cup, his soul the wine therein, Flesh is a pipe, spirit the voice within; O Khayyam, have you fathomed what man is? A magic lantern with a light therein."

The second difference between East and West, as illustrated in Islam and explained by Joseph Campbell, is the lack of free will as we know it in Western civilization. Rather, consensus is what determines actions, which is to say that individuals conform to whatever Law of God constituted the local, socially-maintained system of sentiments. Disobedience, the exercise of individual judgment and freedom of decision, was exactly Satan's crime.

Campbell states that the chief creative movement in Europe was due to the waning of the priestly mindset. This derived largely from Western civilization's cultural and scientific inheritance from Islam, especially through its branch in Spain. Campbell next quotes Alan Watts, and I paraphrase Watts lightly as saying that myth is a revelation of a timeless event going on within man forever.

Conclusion

In this book, Campbell draws a sharp line between the attitudes toward divinities as exhibited by priests and their followers, and by creative poets, artists, and philosophers. The former group of individuals looks at their divinities through prayer, while the poet realizes that all representation is conditioned by human fallibility. Based on these distinctions above, Campbell defines four functions of mythology. The first is instilling a sense of awe. Secondly, he claims that a myth should create an image of the world fitting for this sense of awe. Third, a myth should support the social order. And, finally, a myth should guide each individual to realize his spiritual fulfillment.

Today, our circle's "circumference is nowhere and its center everywhere; the circle of infinite radius, which is also a straight line." This quote is by Nicholas Cusanus as quoted by Campbell, provenance unknown. Campbell's last thought is a question: "But if there is no divinity in nature, the nature that God created, how should there be in the idea of God, which the nature of man created?" Since I can have the last word, I rephrase Campbell's thought, paradoxically: if there is no divinity on earth, which God created, how can there be divinity in God, which man created?

Chapter Seventeen
Myths to Live By

The book *Myths to Live By* is a series of lectures that Joseph Campbell gave from 1958 to 1971, in which he explores the role of myth in our lives. I'll move through the lectures, again selectively.

In this book, Campbell states that symbols interpreted literally tend to support their civilization's moral order. Without them, according to Campbell, civilizations disintegrate, a claim reminiscent of what Toynbee said in his book *A Study of History*. This opening statement by Campbell sets the tone of his book as well as his own thinking. It also illustrates the problems that many former Soviet citizens have been having since the end of communism in 1990, with their myths destroyed, their beliefs gone, and no anchor to their lives. Yes, we all need myths to live by.

The Old and New Testaments and the Koran are full of apparently historic events. Campbell writes that when these events are denied historicity they become facts of the mind. "Facts of the mind made manifest in a fiction of matter," as Maya Deren phrased the mystery. (The editor of this book wants me to mention where this quote of Deren's comes from, and all I can say about it is she was the aunt of one of my favorite actors at La Mama Theater, Genji Ito, and he gave me this quote from his memory.) The important thing to remember is that the period roughly from 1840 to 1940 was fraught with scientific destruction of old myths without understanding either their import or the need to replace them.

Darwin epitomizes this period, and certainly Freud increasingly dominated it with his theory that myth is public dream, and dream is private myth. A different approach is held by Carl Jung (and me): "In whose views the imageries of mythology and religion serve positive, life-furthering ends." According to Jung, all the organs of our bodies, not just those of sex and aggression, have their purposes and motives, some of which are subject to conscious control while others are not. Our outward-oriented consciousness, addressed to the demands of the day, may lose touch with these inward forces; and the myth is the means to bring us back in touch.

The third section of *Myths to Live By* contains Campbell's lectures about rituals, in which he says that one of the functions of ritual is to give shape to human life. Myths are the spiritual part of rites, whereas rites are the physical part of myth. During my years in East Africa, I watched several rites of passage, the longed-for ritual that changed an adolescent from a dependent into a responsible member of his tribe. But, as Campbell points out, in our Western civilization we ask more of our youth than a passage rite; we ask them to mature as a thinking individual who is also a part of society, thereby fulfilling a creative process.

The key word here is "creative," for we are all caught up today in the increasing pace of change, and without the ability to innovate and to create, we are left behind. Nobody told me that, much less taught me what to expect; the necessity crowded in till change became a way of life, as described in earlier chapters.

Today, in 2007, I am being challenged as never before, and I recognize this challenge to change as the challenge of life itself. Without it there is only death and decay; with change, creative change, there is a choice. Also, there is a need for individual patience; patience for enough time to elapse so that the intent of the change within ourselves is clear and we don't pre-empt the change through overly hasty action.

Campbell's next lecture focuses on the basic difference between East and West, that Western civilization's concern is the individual, whereas the Orient has a disembodied concept of individuals, which I think of as subsumed in society, along similar lines as Campbell's view. This is a vital thought for me, living for five years in Turkey, caught between East and West in such an interesting way. And it is this difference between East and West, between the individual versus the collective, that is evidenced in New York City and Istanbul so strikingly. The violence so palpable on the sidewalks of New York is just as evidently missing among the people of Istanbul.

Perhaps the most explicit thinker on this subject is C. G. Jung with his theory of individuation, or living as a released individual. And, once the individual is made to feel "released," they also become free to vent inner emotions such as anger and fear, whereas the Easterner keeps those emotions within themselves, at least until their human dignity suffers such degradation that they erupt into fundamental violence.

The 1989–92 collapse of communism in the Soviet Union is a significant victory for Western civilization and its "individuation" over the Eastern concept of the collective society. Does this suggest the eventual collapse of communism in China? No, and though I wrote those words in 1992 they are as true today in 2007 as they were fifteen years ago, because the mental set of the Orient is much more evident in Beijing than in Moscow.

Communism, after all, is a product of Western civilization, just as Gandhi's revolution was, and it was basically inimical to Western civilization because it rejects the individual in favor of the collective. Yet this idea is woof and warp to the Orient, and I believe that communism will thrive there despite the fact that a market economy is co-thriving there today in 2007. The reason that they can co-exist is that communism is a part of the Oriental psyche, but the market economy is a part of human nature. They can co-exist, philosophically, in the Orient but could not co-exist in Central Europe or the Soviet Union any more than they could co-exist within me. How about China, you may ask, and I can only reply that their mixture of market economy and communism is only beginning. Ask that question in 2020, and there will be dozens of books published explaining either why it works, or how it failed.

Toynbee suggests that the ultimate answer to disparate traditions or cultures is intermarriage. My personal experience indicates that this is a very slow process that doesn't always work. To be effective, each of us must arrive at our own meaning for each of the symbols our myths present to ourselves. Dogma and tradition defeat this process, overlaying real meaning with someone else's tortured rationale. Many of us today seek gurus instead of teachers; we become unquestioning disciples instead of being led to our own definitions and goals within our own spiritual capacities.

The seventh lecture in Campbell's book talks about Zen. Campbell says there are two types of strength that he defines as kitten and monkey. The kitten's mother cat picks it up when danger threatens and removes it from danger. The monkey in danger leaps on its mother's back and saves itself. Campbell calls these two types "outside strength" and "own strength." Zen is using your own strength, yet Zen is also all things, and therefore is outside strength as well.

All primitive mythologies are of the type that consider conflict and warfare to be good. Most of these rites and mythologies suggest strongly there is no such thing as death; spilled blood returns to mother earth for more life. Campbell suggests that the two greatest books of war mythology in the West are the *Iliad* and the Old Testament.

Then, about 750 BC, a new idea came about as people realized that if they killed everyone in a town or province, there would be nobody left to work the land or to war against. This new realization created the concept of moving a conquered people to a new area and replacing them with others. The most famous members of this uprooted group were the Israelites, who were removed to Babylon from Jerusalem. Almost two hundred years later, Cyrus the Great of Persia took Babylon and sent the Israelites back to Jerusalem and encouraged them to rebuild their temple. These Persians' mythology, or religion, was of Zarathustra, or Zoroaster. And it was this mythology that encouraged Cyrus to return the Israelites to their homeland.

Fundamental to this mythology was the imminent end of the world. Therefore, Cyrus and his followers felt a need to hurry in their return of all uprooted peoples to their original homes. The impact of this mythology on the three Judaic religions was, and still is, enormous. It also could be seen as the world's first indication that a united group of nations just might be the answer.

This should be the end of this chapter on mythology so that we can begin the next chapter, on psychology, but Campbell has a quirky chapter of his own in *Myths to Live By* that is part mythology, part psychology, so I'll quote from it briefly next as a bridge between the two.

Campbell lectures about schizophrenia, and parallels it and the mythological journey of an individual soul.

Psychologically, a schizoid needs to complete this journey, rather than being interrupted and returned to health. In the terms laid out by W. B. Yeats in his play *The Cat and the Moon*, he needs a "blessing" rather than a "cure.". He needs to complete the trip from start to finish. Along the way, he must know that "privation and suffering alone open the mind to all that is hidden to others."

There are two kinds of schizoids: essential and paranoid. Paranoid is crazy, having lost all touch with reality; essential is "shamanistic." All schizophrenics have, by definition of their condition, lost touch with reality, but the primitive shaman exhibits a sense of fundamental accord between his outward and inward lives whereas the paranoid schizophrenic lacks even this grasp on reality. I prefer to think of myself as a modern-day shaman rather than accept the idea that I may just be crazy.

Another way of saying the above is that we must see to it that our mythology, the constellation of signs and signals that we are communicating to our young, will deliver messages qualified to relate them richly and vitally to the environment that is to be theirs for life.

And now, mythology is becoming fact as man walks on the moon. "*Che fai, terra, in cielo? Dimmi, che fai, silenziosa terra?*" (What are you doing, Earth, in the sky? Tell me, what are you doing, silent Earth?) as Giuseppe Ungaretti said in 1959 about the first photo of earth from the moon

Campbell writes about this in his next essay, calling it an outward journey. Whereas

Kant suggested that space and time are the a priori forms of sensibility, I feel that they are also the a posteriori forms of sensibility. Giuseppe Ungaretti wrote so feelingly upon seeing the first picture of our earth from the moon, asking a question that we can answer with Campbell's aid. For the earth is "fooling us out of our limits," thereby giving us impetus to scale higher and higher.

Those of us who lived through those heady times remember the adrenalin rush we all participated in, the soaring thoughts we dreamed would come true in that best of all worlds. But life does not travel in a straight line, either for individuals or for nations, and after the fall of communism it took us in another direction, to yet a different level, and we were brought back to reality by the ugly faces of terrorism and natural disaster.

Conclusion

What does it all mean? What can we do? The next chapter merges mythology, or religion, with psychology, or soul, to seek answers to these age-old riddles. Before we get into the psychology of the psyche, however, it is good to think of the man who started most of this discussion, Plato himself. I think of him often when starting a new train of thought, for he was usually there before me, and has often immensely helped me find my way through a subject to the apparent truth. Plato's first idea in *The Republic* was to look at justice in the community before seeking it in an individual, since it looms larger in the group than in a single person and hence can be more easily identified. I have mixed Plato's concepts with my own earlier in this book, examining the common question while explaining its application to me along side it. Now, as a change that illuminates the issue more clearly, I want to illustrate a point by telling a story, or a myth.

It's a great story, and full of implications for each of us individuals who read it, yet it's not a particularly well-known myth, and exists outside any religion.

Section Four:
Psychology

○ ○

L'uomo comanda il giorno e la donna la notte

—(Man rules the day and woman the night)

Chapter Eighteen
Amor and Psyche

Introduction

It began as I was writing about Arnold Toynbee's monumental *A Study of History*, in which Toynbee went deeply into mythology and its roots in both our past and our present. I began studying mythologists and myths all over again, although I had lived with myths and mythology all my life. Inevitably, I chose an American, Joseph Campbell, as my main source around whom I would both read and write. And it was within that framework that I began to understand that in order to fully comprehend what myth means to us today, I would need to better understand psychology, especially what psychologists have written about myth. This process narrows the process to the greats, such as Jung and Kerenyi, as well as to Jung's disciple Erich Neumann, and I draw on these authors for this section.

The more I discovered about the infrastructure of mythology, the more I realized that a thorough comprehension of the feminine was the base. Kerenyi and Jung first lead me to that conclusion, but it is Erich Neumann who substantiates the conclusion so thoroughly that I was further led to a study of most of his writings on the subject, which are legion not only in number but in depth. Some of his depths are nigh inaccessible to the non-psychologist, but well worth the pain of plumbing. (I'm writing this in Firenze, where the "pain of plumbing" is not an idle phrase). My conclusion as I begin writing my thoughts about their thoughts is that the key to this sought-after understanding lies in Neumann's little book *Amor and Psyche*, a detailed version of the old myth first written by Apuleius almost two millennia ago.

Most of us can tell the story simply, but Apuleius wrote a much longer version than the one I learned in school, and Neumann reveals his intentions in the retelling with his subheading "The Psychic Development of the Feminine." I'll begin this chapter with a rather long retelling of the Apuleian myth in my own words, then work into Neumann's psychic development of the feminine, using that as a base for all the further reading and writing. In a way, I'll then be using Neumann as a base, and Jung and Kerenyi will be building on what their follower wrote. I think this approach is as valid as examining Freud through Jung is.

Neumann is a product of his times, as we all are, and his times are the 1930s through the 50s (he died in Tel Aviv in 1960). He was but fifty-five years old when he died, and lacked the experience and time to evaluate his life's experiences. If Neumann had lived as long as his mentor Jung did, he might have contributed as insightfully as Jung did.

Throughout this chapter I shall use the Greek names rather than mix in the Roman equivalents, as Apuleius did. Neumann writes "it is the mighty, primordial god Eros, and not Amor or Cupid" with whom we're dealing. The name Psyche is beautiful because it encompasses, in Greek and Italian, many of my favorite images. Etymologically, the Greek verb means to "breathe," hence Psyche becomes both soul and butterfly.

The Myth

A king and queen had three daughters: two lovely ones, but humanly so, and then Psyche, so lovely she appeared divine. And as a result, humans began viewing her as divine, neglecting Aphrodite in her temples and shrines. Divine Aphrodite had a very human temper, and she swore vengeance on Psyche. Aphrodite commanded her son Eros to enflame Psyche with one of his magic arrows to love the vilest of men, "one whom fortune has condemned to have neither health nor wealth nor honor; one so broken that through all the world his misery has no peer" (Apuleius).

Eros, instead, fell in love with Psyche and wafted her gently to his castle in a hidden vale, where he made her his willing bride. But Eros only made love to Psyche at night, in the dark, and she saw him not, although she felt him and talked with him. And one night he told her that her parents were distressed at her probable death, and that her sisters would come to the nearby crags overlooking their valley. But, Eros insisted, Psyche could not answer her sisters' laments, or she would regret it. And Psyche began to understand that she was in a golden prison, and she wept, and wept again. So Eros relented, saying "You may see your sisters, and reassure them, but beware, for the penalty will be large, the punishment sure."

Psyche commanded the west wind to bring her sisters from the crags above, and they arrived and were astonished at the power and wealth that Psyche had. And they were consumed with envy as Psyche loaded them with jewels and gold, yet she was most indefinite about her husband, the source of all the wealth.

Envy gnawed at the two sisters, even as the west wind wafted them home. Eros cautioned Psyche, saying "those false she-wolves are weaving some deep plot of sin against you, and they will torment you to see my face, which, if you do, you will never see again." Eros concluded: "Even now your womb bears a child like to you. If you keep my secret in silence, he shall be a god; if you divulge it, a mortal." And Eros warned Psyche yet again of her sisters' planned treachery, yet Psyche begged to see them once more, and once more Eros relented.

So the west wind wafted the cruel sisters to Psyche once more, and they began weaving their web of deceit and charm. And they did sow doubt in Psyche's soul. That very night, Psyche lighted her lamp and at last gazed on the forbidden form of Eros as he slept. And her heart rejoiced at his beauty as she fondled his arrows, one of which pricked her finger, causing her to fall hopelessly in love with Love.

But a drop of hot oil from her lamp fell on Eros, awakening him to her betrayal, and he took off with scarce a fare-thee-well to poor Psyche. Psyche, realizing the evil her sisters had wrought on her, visited one, saying: "Eros reviled me when I beheld his beauty, saying he was leaving me forever and would marry you, my sister." That sister immediately ran to the crag and jumped off, commanding the west wind to bear her to Eros.

And then Psyche dispatched her other sister in like manner, leaving their entrails entwined on the rocks that bestrew the valley.

And now Aphrodite was sorely angered, for she had told her son Eros to marry Psyche to a wretch, and instead this wretched son had married Psyche himself.

Heaven hath no fury like a goddess scorned, and Eros felt the whips and scorns of outraged divinity as his mother swore to clip both his wings and his hair, depriving him of beauty and power in her rage. Meanwhile, Psyche appealed to Demeter directly, but was repulsed, saying she could not and would not so offend her fellow goddess Aphrodite. Psyche next appealed likewise to Hera, who rejected her in like words.

Aphrodite was seeking Psyche high and low to punish her further, and enlisted Hermes' help. So poor Psyche was brought before Aphrodite, who reviled her and had her scourged, saying: "Behold, she thinks to move me with pity because she is big with child, and the time is near when the fair fruit of her womb shall make me a happy grandmother. Truly, I am highly blessed that I should be called a grandmother, though yet in the flower of my age, and that the son of a vile serv-ing-wench should be known as Aphrodite's grandchild! But I am a fool to call him her son. He is no true son, for the parties to the marriage were not of equal birth, while the wedding took place in a country house unwitnessed and without the father's consent. It cannot therefore be regarded as legitimate, and the child will be born a bastard, at least if we allow you to become a mother at all."

And she condemned Psyche to sort out an impossible mountain of assorted beans. Psyche's bean problem was easily resolved by a horde of miraculous ants. Aphrodite next sent Psyche to gather golden wool, knowing that Psyche would die if she did. Yet another deus ex machina arrived in the form of a reed, telling Psyche how to overcome the challenge. Leaning on that slender reed, Psyche overcame. Aphrodite then challenged Psyche to bring her an urn filled with icy waters from "yonder lofty cliff." And yet another deus stepped ex machina in bird form and fetched the required waters.

Aphrodite laid yet a fourth task on poor Psyche: to go to Hades and bring back some of Persephone's magic beauty. The final deus is a tower of a machina that babbles all to Psyche. The details were devilish, but by now Psyche had some idea that she was being watched over, not by one of the main deities (at least not openly), for these had turned her down, but perhaps by a myriad of lesser ones.

Psyche's own cupidity was stronger than her desire for Eros, and she couldn't resist looking in the casket when she arrived above ground after Hades. Only Sleep was within, and Psyche was enveloped.

Now Psyche was blessed by yet another deus ex machina, this time the same one that first seduced her, Eros himself, restored from his wound and his mother, and who next petitioned Zeus himself to end Aphrodite's trials of both Psyche and Eros. Following this successful venture, Psyche gave birth to a daughter, and "in the language of mortals she is called 'Pleasure.'"

The Psychic Development of the Feminine: Commentary

Psyche's father was advised by Apollo's oracle to abandon Psyche on "some high crag" to await a bridegroom not of mortal seed, but "fierce and wild of the dragon breed." When Psyche is taken away by Eros, who she sees not, her sisters convince her that she is indeed married to a wild and fierce dragon.

Yet the basics go beyond the story, for the clash is neither with her sisters nor between Eros and Psyche, but between Aphrodite and Psyche, and it derives from Aphrodite's birth from the severed penis of Uranus being thrown into the Aegean Sea from whence she arose from the foam on the half-shell, as she was immortalized by Botticelli.

By contrast, Psyche, the "new Aphrodite," was born of the earth impregnated by a drop of heaven's dew. Both Neumann and I believe that the conflict between Aphrodite and Psyche is central to the myth, and I shall stress it further than he does because I believe that Neumann tends to weaken the bond through omission.

Why do I leave Eros out of the title of this myth? Because I feel that he is but an instrument of Aphrodite's will, even when he disobeys that will. He's as much a secondary, albeit necessary, character as Hades is in the Demeter-Persephone myth. And in both myths in somewhat different guises we see the rape aspect of marriage, as evidenced by the male husband separating the daughter from her mother, abducting her, and acquiring her, or raping her.

From the female's viewpoint the above represents "destiny, transformation and the profoundest mystery of life," according to Neumann in *Amor and Psyche*. I prefer the former, especially when the above is interpreted through the myth of Persephone and Hades, which is better titled the myth of Demeter and Persephone, as we'll see a few pages on. Neumann describes the act of defloration as representing a "mysterious bond between end and beginning, between ceasing to be and entering upon a real life" to a woman. I believe that this is a simplification, and Demeter—Persephone, especially when they speak with one voice, are the real representatives of womanhood, as I will explain further when I write more on them.

Both marriage and childbirth are archetypal experiences, but do not actually require the individual to go through the physical process consciously. This concept is a marriage of Jung's thoughts on Demeter-Persephone and Neumann's on Aphrodite-Psyche. And this is what the myth of Psyche begins with, for it appears that Psyche is not conscious as she accepts the oracle's telling her to go to a lofty crag to await a monster, where instead Eros appears and has her wafted to his paradisiacal castle and garden.

Psyche still seems unconscious as she welcomes the "serpent in the garden," namely her sisters, who provide her, Eve-like, with the wherewithal to be expelled from the garden. Neumann digs into these sisters, for they are truly psychological manipulators, even more so than the serpent they represent. First, both of them hate their husbands and are ready to leave them. Neumann says that their marriages "are a symbol of patriarchal slavery." Further, "both sisters are intense man-haters and represent a typical position of the matriarchate."

The sisters next tell Psyche to kill her husband by cutting off his head with a knife, "an ancient symbol of castration sublimated to the spiritual sphere." Once more these words suggest Aphrodite's parentage from Uranus' severed penis. Psyche rises above her previous unconsciousness as a result of her sisters' visits, seeing her life with Eros as a "luxurious prison."

Psyche's life with Eros is a state of yin, and her sisters represent a force from outside that enables her to leave her unconscious yin state and become consciously creative in the yang state, which is necessarily outside of paradise.

And here Neumann sees the essence of their relationship: Eros is indeed the non-human monster foretold by Apollo's oracle and Psyche is his victim. The disgrace of Psyche succumbing to Eros can only be eradicated by her killing and castrating the masculine, a la Judith in the Old Testament. And Neumann gets to the heart of the matter as he quotes Psyche revealing her inner situation: "I seek no more to see your face; not even the dark of night can be a hindrance to my joy, for I hold you in my arms, light of my life."

Just as Psyche appears to accept Eros and his love in all the strangeness of his demands, she admits to a deeper desire to see and know her lover. In effect, she changes dramatically from darkness to light, from her basic state of yin to a yearning for yang. She is changing her lifestyle as she undergoes self-knowledge and suddenly rejects the very concept of Eros just as she appears to accept him most wholeheartedly.

This is a most strange metamorphosis as she becomes more human and less divine, and establishes herself as the true protagonist she is meant to be. Eros we can overlook, for he is numinous, an archetype, albeit exhibiting some modestly human traits as he begins to humanly love Psyche.

As we center on Psyche, it equally becomes apparent that her counterpart in this myth is not Eros, but his mother Aphrodite. Psyche is no longer the simple and simple-minded girl portrayed in the myth, but a very complex, interesting, and intelligent person. At the start of Apuleius' myth, she seems cold and unapproachable, like the princess in Puccini's opera *Turandot*. Unlike Turandot, however, Psyche warms up, slowly, like a bud unfolding, as she becomes human. When? When she stops being a zero, a non-human yet non-divine being, about the time she tells her first sister to jump into Eros' arms.

This is truly an awakening of the conscious in Psyche, as she becomes human. I would like to know the person she becomes at this point. She has now started to taste life, and has made her own salt therein. She's not just human, she's interesting, at least until Apuleius' false ending when she becomes divinely uninteresting.

Imagine how glorious Psyche could be, could have been, if she'd achieved her apotheosis in a real way instead. For example, instead of becoming a goddess in a divine wedding, she might have overcome her arrow-induced love for Eros and mutilated him, reducing him permanently from Eros to Cupid. She even could have taken on Aphrodite directly, and beat her, for Psyche was a crusader and, let loose, could have initiated her own era's Götterdämmerung by doing in Aphrodite.

How would this have happened? Mutilating Eros would have stunted Aphrodite's psyche more than Eros' penis, to say nothing of its effect on Eros' putative father Zeus. Back to the moment of opportunity: Psyche approaches the sleeping Eros, knife in hand as well as light, meaning that she had both the knowledge and the ability to mutilate. But Psyche sees Eros as a god instead of a dragon, and she turns the knife inward upon herself, instead of toward Eros.

Neumann describes this moment as "what Psyche now experiences may be said to be a second defloration, which she accomplishes in herself. She is no longer a victim, but an actively loving woman. She is in love, enraptured by Eros, who has seized her as a power from within, no longer as a man from without."

Neumann and I differ about the interpretation of Psyche's act, although we agree on its import. Neumann says that Psyche's act creates within her an Eros far different from the Eros sleeping there outside her. Psyche's unconscious tendency towards consciousness is stronger than her love for Eros. But it is in light of this new love that Psyche approaches consciousness. At the same time, Psyche also deprives Eros of power over her, and they now confront one another as equals. And on this new plane of consciousness and love Psyche transcends the separation accomplished by her act.

Here something should be said about the symbolism of the scalding oil that burns Eros. "Ah, rash, overbold lamp," says our tale, "thou burnest the very lord of fire." But what causes the suffering is not a knife or sword, but the oil itself. Neumann sees the oil in this situation as "significant as the basis of light, and to give light it must burn." Similarly in psychic life, it is the heat, the fire of passion, the flame and the ardor of emotion, that provide the basis of illumination; that is, of an illumined consciousness, which rises from the combustion of the fundamental substance and enhances it. Gods do not suffer; suffering is as human as love is, and gods only experience desire and pleasure, like animals.

Gods may experience things unconsciously, but since they are archetypes themselves they lack the ability to be conscious. Another example is in Wagner's operatic *Ring Cycle*, where Wotan approaches consciousness when he understands his daughter, Brunnhilda. His consciousness conflicts with his divinity, or status as archetype, and in this conflict he becomes closer to being human, thereby signaling the twilight of the gods.

Psyche's new job is to hold onto her own grasp of consciousness since it is her password out of paradise, which is in fact Hades and a life of unconsciousness. She is becoming herself, her own self, and this is worth more than Eros to her, and she is conscious of it.

Her second job is to bring Eros to consciousness also; that is, to change him from an archetypal divinity into a human being. Eros accomplished the first part of this move toward consciousness by pricking himself with one of his arrows and falling in love with Psyche. Now he needs Psyche's help to rise above his own divinity.

And here Neumann and I agree totally, as he says "Psyche's act leads to all the pain of individuation, in which a personality experiences itself in relation to a partner as something other, as not only connected to the partner." The background of the myth is the conflict between Aphrodite and Psyche, where Neumann's phrase for Aphrodite is the Great Mother, also the title of his masterpiece, which I'll discuss separately. Neumann refers frequently to Aphrodite's depiction as a fertility goddess, or earth mother, whose chief purpose is fertility of humans, animals, and plants.

During the five years when I lived and worked in Anatolia, I visited the great museums and sites of Turkey, seeing the very early fertility symbols firsthand. The ten-thousand-year-old seated figures of pregnant women in the Ankara museum, for example, are some of the first representations of fertility worship, indicating that the first religions were matriarchal. Therefore, Psyche's conflict with Aphrodite went to the source of power, fertility itself, which is why Psyche now dominates the action: not just because she is proceeding from unconsciousness to consciousness, but because she is pregnant.

As Neumann confirms, it is this fertility that gave the first earth mother her dignity, "the queenship by virtue of which she invested the king with his power."

Aphrodite plans to destroy Psyche through the four labors that she imposes on her. These labors seem strange, and as impossible for a human to perform as Heracles' were, but each labor tests Psyche's resolve anew and in a different way.

The labors are imposed from outside of Psyche and her world, and represent a true test, from each direction of the compass, of her humanity, or of her passing from the unconscious to the conscious, from yin to yang. Neumann sees the four labors as symbols of the unconscious. He describes the first labor sorting out the seeds as representing a uroboric mix of the masculine. I think that this may be far-fetched, an attempt to somehow explain this labor in psychological terms, but I can agree with Neumann that Psyche does bring order to the promiscuity of the seeds, and her order, or selecting, is a human trait.

In the second labor, Aphrodite sends Psyche to disarm the solar, or masculine, power, much as Delilah did to Samson, or Judith to Holofernes, or Salome to John: a symbolic castration. Aphrodite's planned ruin of the feminine, represented by Psyche, is averted through the providential help of a reed, a symbol of both earth and sun. The solution, presented by the reed, is one of patience: wait till nightfall, as Neumann says.

The third labor uses water as a uroboric stream that is essentially uncontainable, and Psyche's labor, as a feminine vessel, is to contain the male-generative stream. Neumann sees significance in the use of Zeus' eagle as the deus ex machina since it is a masculine symbol apparently being used with Zeus' permission to help contain the masculine stream of life. Further, Neumann sees the eagle of Ganymede being specifically used to stress the homoerotic aspect of this labor, for this type is "important in the war of liberation against domination by the Great Mother."

Also, Eros must be free of Aphrodite's domination before he can "enter into a free and independent relation with Psyche." Further, Psyche now has a male-female spirituality symbolized by the eagle holding the vessel. Since she is earth-born, she can only accomplish things with her reach, but "this precisely is what befits her and makes her human."

In her fourth labor, Psyche is no longer struggling with the masculine principle, but rather with Aphrodite herself. And the symbol, the deus ex machina that comes to her aid, is both masculine and feminine, for a tower is both a phallus and the crown of the feminine godhead. And now Psyche yields to human curiosity and is overwhelmed with a death-like sleep. This last labor, or trick, of Aphrodite's fails because "Psyche is not concerned with the fertility of nature, which is the only thing that interests Aphrodite, but with the fertility of individual encounter."

And this is not just a failure of Aphrodite versus Psyche, but of East versus West, the collective versus the individual. Eros' humanity is not central to the myth, but Psyche's growth to consciousness is. "Psyche must not simply travel through the elements, she must make them her own through her acts of sufferings and assimilate them as the helpful forces of her nature." This is the mystery of Eleusis. Now we reach the end, a happy one, apparently, for Psyche and Eros, but a strangely forced and unsatisfactory one for me.

Psyche has achieved great things through her humanity, through her non-divinity. Her progression from unconsciousness to consciousness is a triumph of the psychic development of the feminine, and especially a personal triumph for Psyche the woman, the individual human being. Her apotheosis should be the humanizing of Eros, and hence a twilight of the gods. But no, she gives up her hard-won humanity and Eros keeps his divinity despite becoming a bit human, and, alas, they have a divine child. Neumann disagrees with me in this interpretation, saying instead that "when Psyche is received into Olympus as the wife of Eros, an epoch-making development of the feminine and all humanity is manifest in myth. Seen from the feminine viewpoint, this signifies that the soul's individual ability to love is divine, and that transformation by love is a mystery that deifies. This experience of the feminine psyche takes on special importance against the background of the ancient patriarchal world with its collective feminine existence, subordinated to the rule of the fertility principle."

Neumann has done a great job of presenting this myth and explaining it in psychological terms that break new ground. I believe that he winds up with several strings in hand that simply do not match, and he forces them to comply. He sees that Psyche won against the forces of Aphrodite because she, Psyche, was human, and he sees further that Psyche goes beyond what the gods are, or can be, at least as her own society saw them.

This holds true for both Psyche's time and for Apuleius', but Neumann takes these thoughts and tries to resolve them too quickly, ending with the weak resolution that "the human bond with the divine is not only eternal, but itself of a divine quality." This is the old dodge of answering about a difficult problem by saying that "you have to trust me because the answer is a matter of unprovable faith." No, the true answer is that the whole system of gods was wrong, as Psyche proved through her humanity, and she won both the battles and the war because she did not compromise her humanity. The end of the story should instead have seen Psyche complete her conquest of Eros' divinity by making him fully human.

Apuleius' myth of Aphrodite and Psyche must have been strongly influenced by the concept of Prometheus bringing divine gifts to mankind. The widespread acceptance of this idea some 2,500 years ago had so permeated the Mediterranean culture five hundred years later that Apuleius had only to refer to it off-handedly to be fully understood by his audience. For Apuleius the experience of religious initiation became the personal experience of mankind, indicating that he was one of those creative people who, like the feminine, must give "birth"; one of those "whom Psyche guides."

Before reviewing Erich Neumann's masterpiece *The Great Mother,* I want to insert some thoughts of his teachers, both Kerenyi and Jung, since they informed Neumann's ideas about *The Great Mother.*

Chapter Nineteen
Essays on a Science of Mythology

Carl Kerenyi and C. G. Jung collaborated in writing this book about myth, with Kerenyi analyzing the Divine Child and Maiden myths in order to show the meaning of myths to the myth-makers and Jung talking about what it means to the inner world or psyche.

Kerenyi and Jung agree that myth is the common denominator between poetry and religion. Kerenyi defines myth as something alive, moving, and growing: "It is something solid and yet mobile, substantial and yet not static, capable of transformation." Also, like music, myth, or "mythologem," as Kerenyi prefers, it's something you just live with and absorb (*Essays on a Science of Mythology*).

This is what the Catholic Church tried to become to its followers: a source of endless mythologems offering not just a pattern for life, but a way to make each believer's life have meaning. Yet when I was with a close relative during the last few months of his long life, he leaned heavily on his Catholic religion to help him achieve a dignified death, only to find it a broken reed, a compass that wavered meaninglessly. How could I intrude on this nightmare in a meaningful way? I thought that I knew some answers; I could have read to him from *The Prophet*. But his family and especially his priests would have been horrified at my attempts to bring philosophic solace to a Catholic, and thus he died as if free falling in the void, with no support.

If I were to change a religion to make it more satisfying to the dying, I would take *The Prophet*'s words on death as a starter and add to them Plato's words on death as he put them in Socrates' mouth, and then fashion some myths about the actual passing of a body from life to death, stressing the freeing of the soul to fulfill itself through the death process.

The question we all must face is how will we react when we know that we are about to die? I think that I know my own answer, although I cannot be sure until the moment arrives, when it will probably be too late to write about it. This book contains all that I have thought about and learned in life, after nearly eighty years, and it represents my attitude toward both life and death.

I shall paraphrase Kerenyi in my own words to clarify the next statement since the translator, or Kerenyi himself, has used confusing pronouns and tenses, and far too much Greek language:

What are those things in which I can really find myself? To which of them can I dive down straightaway? They are as numerous as the elements composing my world, including myself. I have my own core, the center of my organic being from which I continually create myself. As a developed organism, I experience my own origin thanks to a kind of identity, as though I am a reverberation of it multiplied a thousandfold and my origin was the first note struck.

I experience this as my absolute core, a beginning since when I was a unity fusing in itself all the contradictions of my nature and life to be. It is an immersion in myself that leads to the living germ of my wholeness, where the relative and absolute coincide. The absolute is my origin; the relative is my "relatives," i.e., my immortality through both my progenitors and my children.

Kerenyi next states that ritual is a translation of myth into an act. He makes the recurring point that myth is not biography; but then he qualifies that by saying mythology is actually both of these things, "more or less." What he seems to be saying is that mythology depicts the timeless quality of the gods, so it is not biographical even when it tells a story about a specific incident in a god's life.

I prefer to accept the literal meaning of "bio" as life and use that as my base. Kerenyi asks us readers what affects us in myth, and answers himself that it is divinity revealed. A fairly original thought, but I disagree with his conclusion. He next asks us which came first, the human condition or the original mythologem? He considers, like Plato, that the original mythologem pre-existed in what he terms the "primordial." Yet how could it? It is human reason that originated the mythologem, even though it might have its cause in our genes, or some primordial common instincts within us. But without the human mind to ponder this mythologem, it would not exist, QED.

Jung takes Kerenyi's ideas, and mine, to new levels through science. He relates that several patients, who could have had no access to mythology, had "typical mythologems" observed among them. Jung's conclusion was that "myth-forming structural elements must be present in the unconscious psyche." Jung calls these "motifs," or "archetypes," and says "archetypes appear in myths and fairy tales just as they do in dreams and in the products of psychotic fantasy."

He continues, adding that archetypes' meanings can only be guessed at, whereas myth is of a more traditional form. I traced many such myths as I researched my thesis in Kenya over several years, finding that people steeped in oral tradition only (meaning that they are illiterate), are especially gifted with large memories. My work there was during the late 1960s and early 1970s, and most of those people have since died; with ubiquitous schools and literacy, nobody has replaced them with knowledge and retention of oral tradition.

Jung had little direct contact with people who only had oral tradition, and hence he claims that, in the case of such an individual, "owing to the chronic twilight state of his consciousness, it is often next to impossible to find out whether he merely dreamed something or whether he really experienced it." This sounds like a reasonable interpretation, but I lived with these people for over two years in the high hills in western Kenya, and I discovered it easy to tell when my interviewees were telling me a fact, even though it occurred several hundred years ago, or when they were making it up. The process is really just a matter of getting to know the people by living with them and having them trust you

I took a subject, for example, such as why men from one tribe were forbidden to marry a woman from the same tribe. "Ah, ha" said I, recalling the word "exogamous" that describes this condition, but which I'd never spoken before, much less encountered. I thought I knew exactly why the tribal law was instituted, probably either to keep the tribal gene pool filled up, or maybe for the fun of having the tribe's young men perform a daring feat by carrying off a foreigner. The reason known by the tribespeople themselves was usually something else, having little connection with my preconceived notions.

The above situation could be serious, or only partly so: although such a marriage would be taboo to that tribe, if a young man strongly desired to marry within his tribe, and his tribe was large enough, the rule or taboo could be breached, depending on many circumstances. Sometimes, after I had the confidence of the people, they would even ask my opinion in a certain case, which is why I learned as many of their proverbs as possible, for there was always at least one of them that would apply to the situation at hand. I feel certain today that had Jung had the time and opportunity to live with these oral tradition people, he would have been fascinated by the potential ramifications to his theories.

Jung's feelings about myth run deep, and he believed that they constitute the psychic life of the tribe, and, further, that when myths are lost to a tribe, the tribe decays. I agree, especially after witnessing firsthand the collapse of communism in the early 1990s, leaving many of its adherents bereft, unbelieving, enveloped in a "moral catastrophe."

Jung describes two categories of unconscious fantasy activity, including dream: those of a personal character, related to personal experiences, and impersonal ones, not related to personal experiences. These latter are mythological types, corresponding to collective elements or inherited ones. Jung calls these "autochthonous revival," and they are so numerous that he thinks they form a substratum he then called the collective unconscious. He then defined the self as the wholeness that transcends consciousness, and the synthesis of the self becomes the individuation process.

This is why the child motif in mythology is important, for it symbolizes this process of synthesis from its beginning, or childhood. Yet all these child myths also stress the divine. Each father in these myths is a god, such as Zeus himself, Hermes, Apollo, and so on. Each also overcomes early adversities such as abandonment and persecution. As divine, each personifies the collective unconscious. The hero, on the other hand, being part human, like Hercules, has a main feat to overcome the monster of darkness (unconsciousness), such as Siegfried's dragon.

When the apparent protagonist of Wagner's operatic *Ring Cycle* does this, and tastes the dragon's blood, symbolizing the triumph of consciousness over unconsciousness, he suddenly "knows," gains instant insight, and can "hear" what the birds of nature are saying to him. His consciousness has triumphed, but he is still a childlike human.

Siegfried's earlier abandonment symbolizes the "horror vacui" of the unconscious, "which is quite ready to swallow up all its progeny, since it produces them only in play, and destruction is an inescapable part of its play." Yet the abandonment is necessary, since "child means something evolving towards independence. This it cannot do without detaching itself from its origins." Yet Siegfried never achieves higher consciousness, which is "knowledge going beyond our present-day consciousness and is equivalent to being alone in the world," and he dies a relative child (Jung).

Conclusion

Jung's conclusion is that psychology takes ancient myths and transliterates them into today's language and understanding.

The Kore

The third chapter of the *Science of Mythology* talks about the kore. Botticelli's picture of Venus should be in our minds as we think of the kore, or maiden: Aphrodite rising from the sea, the foam, her father's mutilated penis and all, is the essence of the maiden.

Divinities were believed in as living gods, but Kerenyi says that they are best understood as forms or ideals, or eternal truths, much as Plato described in *The Republic*. Kerenyi suggests thinking of these truths, or myths, as something yet unopened, like a bud. All of the old myths are buds like this. This bud-like quality is inherent in the name "kore," or "maiden."

Well, "maiden" really suggests to us in the twenty-first century West a woman not yet married, whereas in Kerenyi's and Jung's writings it signifies a woman who has not yet had a child. An older way to think of a kore is to consider her bud-like capacity as also containing a whole world in itself: the capacity to create life.

Kerenyi goes back in time to the central myth of Persephone's rape by Hades. Persephone, Demeter's daughter, was also known as Kore because she was the personification of all the korai, and her rape by Hades was an allegory of a death that was necessary for her to assume her other identity as Queen of the Dead. This suggests to me another form of death: that of the spirit.

Kerenyi examines the Homeric hymn to Demeter, who is often pictured holding an ear of grain. He says that Demeter does not show what to do with the grain, but the answer is contained in the overall Mystery of Eleusis. Demeter represents, in the Eleusinian Mysteries, the power inherent in motherhood, fecundity realized, symbolized by the ear of grain. The negative of this aspect is death, represented by Persephone's rape and her role as Queen of the Dead, and also by winter, the time when she takes on this role.

Kerenyi expands on the aspect of the ear of grain, for it can be made into food by putting it in the fire (perhaps the fire of Hades?). It is also the symbol of the oneness of mother and daughter. For Kerenyi, Demeter represents the "universal principle (as well as principal) of life, which is to be pursued, robbed, raped, to fail to understand, to rage and grieve, but then to get everything back and to be born again."

The initiates of the Eleusinian Mysteries identified themselves with Demeter, this universal principle of life. In other words, the initiate entered into divine motherhood, not unlike the Christian becoming Christ-like through the sacrament of communion. The principal thing in Eleusis is that "birth is a more-than-individual phenomenon, through which the individual's mortality was perpetually counterbalanced, death suspended, and the continuance of the living assured." In another word: immortality.

The Psychological Aspects of the Kore

Next, Jung addresses the psychological aspects of the kore concept. Jung sees the possibility of duplication in psychic figures; at least, they move between positive and negative freely.

He further feels that myths were not consciously created. Toward the end of Jung's life, he witnessed Hitler's invention of myths. If a myth is consciously invented, is it therefore false?

I think not, for Hitler's myths were consciously invented and were knowingly false, yet they were true to their cause: Nazism. No matter how hateful the idea, the truth of this falsity insists that these myths were yet true to their cause.

Jung states that motherhood induces a feeling of being tied to both past and future generations, and therefore the sense of a kind of immortality. The individual mother's life assumes meaning in this context. Jung suggests that most professionals don't know enough about their patients' archetypal material. The archetypal material is "the great unknown," and its context is all-important: "What Perseus has to do with the Gorgon's head would never occur to anyone who did not know this myth."

Jung's Conclusion

The essence of Demeter and Kore, or Persephone, is outside the male-female experience; it is mother-daughter only, and derives from the matriarchy and the time before our present-day patriarchy came into being. When did that change take place? Around the same time that Orestes avenged his father's death by killing his mother.

The Miracle of Eleusis

Kerenyi has the last word, and he discusses the Miracle of Eleusis. The initiates of Eleusis paid homage to two goddesses, mother and daughter. Beyond this is speculation, albeit "scientific" speculation. Kerenyi says that we lack direct witness by an initiate, at least so far. He quotes Otto's main question: "How is it that Demeter comes to have this daughter?" Indeed, what does it mean that she is so closely connected with a daughter at all? Otto compares the relations of other daughters to their divine parents and finds none of them so intimate.

An apparent answer to this question was found recently on the sacred isle of Delos in the form of an inscription, stating explicitly that the Eleusinian Demeter was kore and mature woman in one, something I already sensed. I think it was 1978 when I spent four and a half months in Greece, two weeks at each major archeological site, always staying in apartments so that I could cook for myself and avoid the poisonous stew found ubiquitously in Greek restaurants. Why? Because every time a Greek learns to cook they go to Astoria, the second largest Greek city in the world, and also an integral part of New York City.

During my two weeks on Mikonos I ferried to nearby Delos because it had just become possible to stay the night there, something that had previously been forbidden because of the ancient proscription that the world would end if anyone either died or gave birth on Delos. During the night I spent there the world did end for at least a thousand mosquitoes. Arising at five am, just as the mosquitoes passed the baton to the daytime flies, I climbed the small hill with a temple to Apollo on it in order to watch the sunrise. I felt so many mysteries stirring on that tiny isle, more during the day than at night, but adding up to an impressive total. Among them is the feeling that Demeter and Persephone are one.

Was this a dream? Or intuition? Or a direct gift from the gods? I don't know, but I have always felt strong thoughts in situ. I read all the great Greek myths that summer in situ, and had the strongest feeling of all at the Peloponnesian crossroads where Oedipus confronted his father. I shiver in the heat of an Aegean summer right now at the memory.

Is this confirmation of Demeter's oneness? Not really, not objectively, but I think that when you have had direct experiences at both Delos and Delphi, then you are entitled to comment, albeit subjectively.

Kerenyi suggests that the idea of the individual dying while living on in their descendants was something the Eleusinian Mysteries not only imparted as knowledge, but that the initiate partook in, as mentioned above, and became a part of.

To recapitulate my own conclusion, the core of the Eleusinian Mystery is two-fold: the mother-daughter being one aspect, inferring immortality; and the rape-death concept being central to the act of passing from daughter to mother. If the initiate can encompass both of these ideas, whether they are male or female, then they are indeed "initiate," and ready to be initiated into life, or consciousness.

Chapter Twenty
The Great Mother

"A green jewel is my heart, but I will see gold."

—*A song of the Aztec god Xipe*

The above quote from the last pages of *The Great Mother* sums up many of Erich Neumann's thoughts about the subject, including a suggestion that the real alchemy is not to turn bronze (green) into gold metal, but to turn the green of spring into harvest gold. After exploring the myths of Demeter and Persephone and Amor and Psyche, Erich Neumann's *The Great Mother* is a logical step forward. Personally, I am concerned with my own psychological wholeness, and I would like to marry my consciousness to my unconsciousness, my animus to my anima, my yin to my yang. In order to discover the depths of my unconscious, or anima, I need to know more about the Great Mother, and Neumann's book is good because it tells most of what this archetype is and possesses, both good and bad.

Neumann defines the Great Mother as an "inward image at work in the human psyche." An example of archetype at work would appear to a hunter armed lightly seeing a huge bear approaching. An archetypal image of fright and flight would present itself to the hunter's mind, and he would flee, with fear giving wings to his feet. His unconscious would intrude these symbols on his consciousness. This action contrasts with a more primitive hunter who lacks consciousness as we know it. Preconscious people used rites of entry and departure, for example, to imitate the later use of the unconscious to activate the conscious.

Preconscious people must have acted much as Jean Auel describes them in her *Clan of the Cave Bear* series of books. I had read about this behavior in my anthropological studies, but her novels made those ideas come alive. For example, a rite a preconscious person might use would be to simply close his eyes and call up an image of a bear, or some other totem or symbol, in order to bring his consciousness to action. A comparison today would be the people who sit watching television for hours daily. Their will is gradually sapped as their minds degenerate below the high school level they once attained. As they sink back to a preconscious level, their ability to interact consciously is so impaired that they are incapable of concrete discussion and thought processes, much less anything abstract, which is literally beyond them.

The above behavior suggests that a societal return to ritual is necessary in order to interact with these people, since weaning them from TV appears less likely. Graduate students could invent rites, such as a specific rite for channel-changing, and practice them on monkeys to see if they could adapt to them.

The Great Mother is about a different sort of symbol and rite. An archetype, by nature, cannot be consciously invented or changed. The ego does not participate in the genesis of either archetype or symbol. The preconscious, or emergingly conscious, peoples, up till the Trojan War for example, tended to see their gods and goddesses as multiple deities. As most emerging peoples were of matriarchal societies, their goddesses were often the embodiment of both light and dark, good and bad. Ishtar, for example, was the goddess of both love and war, and daughter of both day and night.

As their conscious rose and their egos developed, these early peoples came to differentiate their deities. Archetypes are, by their nature, of the earliest sort, combining opposites much as Ishtar represented. I personally connect archetypes per se with the archaic figures of around 500 BC, where the faces were devoid of expression other than a slight smirk. Personalizing an archetype would make it no longer "archaic." This would be akin to Vergil's *Aeneid*, which was both preceded and followed by many other Romans anxious to grind their own axes. I think it a useful and interesting device, but also confusing to mention with archetypes, for they are two different things. Similar to confusing fairy tales with myths, or made-up fairy tales, a la Grimm.

My doctoral work at the University of Nairobi involved me intimately with the Abagusii people of Kenya and especially their leader, Lawrence Sagini, a man my age and size with children that matched mine in age and sex. As the first native Kenyan to be a government minister, Sagini was looked up to by all Kenyans, and he adopted the giraffe as his symbol. Anyone standing for election in Kenya needed some pictographic symbol on the ballot in order for illiterate voters to recognize their candidate. The Swahili word for giraffe is *twiga*, and Sagini became Twiga to his constituents, his fellow tribespeople as well as to all other Kenyans, many of whom did not know his real name.

Sagini followed up on his metaphor, making himself not only a simile for a giraffe, but also associating the giraffe with power and intelligence. All his constituents saw giraffes daily, and knew how powerful and smart they are. I once saw a foreign tourist honk at a giraffe to move it out of the way of his VW Beetle. The giraffe raised one hind leg and squashed that beetle flat.

Sagini told his voters that he would be "like twiga, and eat the best and juiciest leaves from the tops of the trees." This idea appealed to the voters, and many of them told me about it, approving of it. Because of my similar size to Sagini, I also became known as Twiga, although I already had my own totem by then: Ndege, meaning bird.

Neumann gives a thorough and technical definition of the infrastructure of the Great Mother. His main contribution to, or furthering of, Jung's work is the concept of the primordial uroboros, or circular snake that eats his own tail and thereby represents chaos and the unconscious, as well as the psyche, all undifferentiated. This uroboric totality is also a symbol of the parentage of the Great Mother as well as the Great Father. "Thus it is the most perfect example of the still undifferentiated primordial archetype" (*The Great Mother*).

Neumann draws a schema showing the base as the "archetype per se," the first primordial archetype of all, the unconscious. You need to keep in mind both Campbell's and Jung's thoughts on this subject in order to appreciate what Neumann contributes. From the basic archetype per se arises the uroboric Great Mother, which is also the archetypal feminine. And from her arises the Great Mother herself, with defined parts known as Terrible Mother and Good Mother, and taking from both of these arises the anima, all of these representing the unconscious.

At this level the ego appears and then the projected figures, such as human beings, Sophia, Gorgon, and Isis. During maturation, the female's experiences are much sharper than a male's. Menstruation is far more insightful and meaningful than the first issue of sperm in a man. The second blood stage for a woman is birth, with nothing similar for a man.

And now Neumann approaches the core; under a chapter heading entitled "The Central Symbolism of the Feminine," he writes that this central symbol is the vessel. He concludes with a universal equation that woman not only equals the vessel, but also that she equals the world. Everywhere around the Mediterranean Sea I've lived and worked for the past thirty years I find evidence of this, from the ancient Minoan Civilization of over three thousand years ago to present-day Anatolia with its similar "vessels"; from ten thousand years ago in Eastern Turkey to half that long ago in Cycladic Greece; from women with upraised arms suggesting a vessel to the ubiquitous horns of the bull suggesting the same image.

To me, the feminine "vessel" represents the matriarchal millennia that predated our present patriarchy; or, as Jung, Neumann, and Kerenyi say, the "vessel" and matriarchy are representative of the unconscious just as the patriarchy represents consciousness.

Rejection, or deprivation, is opposite to giving, and therefore all distress and privation is from the Great Mother as Terrible Mother. From this concept, Neumann developed the Terrible aspect of the Great Mother into the giver of death, although he considered loneliness to be one of the stronger aspects of her character. Birth is not just release into life, but also a rejection from uterine paradise. It is a progression from yin to yang, as usual from an outer stimulus, and it is a creative process for the individual experiencing it.

Neumann explores the use of alcohol and drugs, along with their resultant stupor and reduction of consciousness, concluding they are all negative. What he does not mention, probably because he didn't know of it or experience it personally, is that a specific, such as champagne, can be either a depressant or a stimulant, depending on the mental set of the drinker.

I have often observed people on a mental descent consume alcohol and merely accelerate their sinking. However, if it is a gloomy Monday in November, nothing improves a rotten day better than sharing a bottle of champagne with a likeminded friend.

Neumann concludes that many mysteries, rites, and doctrines are based on polarity, which the initiate is expected to realize. I never did realize it until reading this book of Neumann's, but years ago, I built a defense against overindulgence. My defense mechanism doesn't always work, but, for example, whereas I once drank alcohol and smoked cigarettes to excess, I have reduced the former to societally accepted levels and eliminated the latter.

Another phenomenon affecting the above, which Neumann ignores, is basic mindset. I am writing this in Taormina, Sicily in early March, 1994, and have had to listen to a gaggle of tourists complain loudly about "endless trifles." On my way to Sicily, I spent most of two days in discussions with bureaucrats in the customs section of Rome's main airport. I was securing the release of a small vial of pills specifically designed to counteract the infection in my mouth from a dentist's ministrations. My face was swollen and I was in obvious discomfort. Precisely at 4:00 PM, ignoring my discomfort as well as my real need, they explained "we close now; come back tomorrow at 10:00."

I learned in childhood not to complain when it accomplishes nothing, so I drove ten minutes to Rome's ancient port, Ostia Antica, extended to magnificence by Emperor Claudius some two thousand years ago. I saw its wonders for the first time and was able to get some photos of the house dedicated to Amor and Psyche, having just finished writing the chapter about them. My memory of those two days is already only of Ostia Antica. My own defense method, an unconscious one, eliminates the bad (but only after taking whatever lesson from it there is to be learned) and retains the good.

In my former home city of Firenze, there is a popular saying "there is no rose without a thorn," or "*non c'e rosa senza spina.*" I prefer to say it the other way round: there is no thorn without a rose. This reversal does more than just turn the saying around; it introduces a new subtlety into it. But the main reason I say it that way is that I try to find the rose when I'm pierced by a thorn.

Because Italians love wordplay and subtlety, this turnaround is appreciated by them, but I've never discussed the reason behind it with them. Now, what has this to do with archetypes and or the Great Mother? Returning to the troubled tourists, they were not afflicted so much with real problems as by ordinary trifles such as we all encounter daily. Because of their concern, they were troubled in their spirit. This confusion on a trifling level frequently leads to one of two things when a real problem or trouble is faced: either the person falls apart in confusion and goes temporarily insane, or else their better character comes forth from the confusion and they suddenly emerge as a leader and solver of problems.

Neumann's conclusion is that a confusion of spirit, or madness, can indeed be taken positively, as I just cited, because behind "inundation by the spirit, the world of archetypes appears as the power that determines fate" (*The Great Mother*). And fate, in all its varying names and guises, is what I've been writing about and practicing all my life, often with disastrous results. My childhood decision to look for the rose derives from my unconscious, from my anima, from the Great Mother herself. A gift of the gods?

Neumann goes back to the early figures of the Great Mother, as illustrated earlier, and "in all of them the symbolism of the rounded vessel predominates. The belly and breasts, the latter often gigantic, are like the central regions of this feminine vessel, the sole reality" (*The Great Mother*).

Neumann doesn't allude to the oldest versions, mostly from Turkey, Syria, and that area, the original Fertile Crescent. I've seen many of these ten-thousand-year-old figures in Ankara's magnificent museum, testifying to the overwhelming numinosity of the earliest women, or great mothers. If you've seen the Mexico City Museum of Wonders, you may think this the best-designed and stocked place in the world to study the history of mankind, but the museum in Turkey's capital, Ankara, is almost as well-designed and accessible, and contains older and more definitive elements that date mankind's historic origins.

Offsetting the positive elements above, are the opposite, or negative, ones. These are the ones that give us our nightmares as they well up from our unconscious through dreams. When I lived in Turkey, I performed an annual ritual expressly designed to illustrate and combat these negative elements.

Following Ramadan is a sacrifice bayram that is ancient in meaning but changed in modern times to indicate a need to change our habits through giving. The rites of the sacrifice are still fairly formal, and require you, the sacrificer, to buy a sheep or goat through an imam, a Muslim priest. The imam brings the ritually cleansed animal to your sacrifice spot, usually your home, and hoists the live beast by its hind legs in front of your door. He cuts its throat, allowing the blood to drain into the earth, thus representing a return of life to whence it came, and also a form of fecundation for the return of new life in the spring, through crops of food or children. It derives from all the early concepts of Persephone returning to her mother, Demeter, each spring in order to cause the new crop season to begin.

This concept is universal, as expressed by such ancient stories as Jonah and the whale, where the sun hero is swallowed anew every evening, and it almost always illustrates the final devouring of all in the earth, mother earth herself, from which all life proceeds and into which all life ultimately descends to be regenerated.

The Transformation Character

In the beginning was chaos, and from it emerged all things; but these first things were dark, whether of earth or heaven. And this primordial darkness of the unconscious preceded the light. Neumann calls this original psychic condition "uroboric" for it contains opposites. He considers this state to be a dynamic one. This dynamic is fire, which can be destructive, but can also be the positive fire of transformation.

Neumann writes lengthily about the Tree of Life, with the feminine character of destiny as both tree and as night. In German legend, Yggdrasil is both heaven in its upper branches and hell in its embracing roots. God hung himself on Yggdrasil for nine days in order to gain true understanding. It was only when he gave one of his eyes that he gained the insight he sought, for only the blind shall truly see. It was this Edda version of God hanging on Yggdrasil that facilitated the Germanic conversion to Christianity because of "the apparent similarity of their hanged god and the crucified Christ."

Neumann dwelt deeply on primitive societies and their beliefs and rites, concluding that they made no connection between the sex act and creating children. Once again, it's easier to understand this concept by reading Jean Auel's extraordinary *Cave Bear* series of books about these primordial people. Her protagonist demonstrates this explicitly in the first book in a way that makes us today appreciate the mindset of our forebears. Neumann goes on from this conclusion to formulate one of his most important contributions to both sociology and anthropology as he claims that male development through battle and the hunt also develops sexual attraction.

He states further that the attendant tension from the attraction described above produced the early social law of exogamy that only allows dissimilar males and females to intermarry. This psychological reason for exogamy is most interesting; I have pondered the various reasons for it among the tribes I lived with in East Africa, realizing its necessity to avoid shallow gene pools, but wondering about the psychology. Today, some of the potential answers are on my doorstep.

I have lived in central Italy in the same small village for eleven years, and I know all the eighty-some villagers, as they know me. Most of them have lived in this village, and married there, for centuries extending into local prehistory. Most houses are obviously centuries old, with additions flaunting their joining scars as families grew. It was only thirty years ago when the path up the hill to our village was made into a road that cars could navigate. That marked the start of education for the children, and also brought electricity and other conveniences such as bottled gas to warm the cold stone houses. Yet, when I arrived, these wonders were new and the old ways, such as intermarriage within the village confines, persisted.

This was so persistent for so long that any sociologist could predict the intelligence level as well as the direction it was headed with the gene pool shallowing out to near idiocy. Yet the actual residents' experience confounds the predictions. For example, a local man and woman are among the first to get an education, and they need to walk several miles downhill each day to get the school bus, and climb back each evening. They learn to read and write, while those just a few years older are still illiterate. This man and woman marry and have three children, a boy and then two girls. Based on the long string of intermarriages within the limited gene pool of the village, the oldest girl, now twenty-three, should have struggled academically to achieve a passing grade through elementary school. Instead, she was the best student in the entire school system of Spoleto, earning a scholarship to the esteemed University of Perugia, where she just graduated as their top student.

If this twenty-three-year-old woman was an exception, we could treat it as such, there are enough other children excelling, where genetics suggests a regression, to make me wonder if there are other, unknown, reasons for this development. It is as if civilization's next Einstein were to be found in a truly isolated village on the upper reaches of the Amazon River.

Perhaps most importantly in this book on the Great Mother, Neumann concludes that "the childbearing virgin, the Great Mother as a unity of mother and virgin, appears in a very early period as the virgin with the ear of grain, the heavenly gold of the stars, which corresponds to the earthly gold of the wheat." This is the key to all that Neumann contributes through this book on the Great Mother: she is Demeter-Persephone, mother and kore, Aphrodite and Psyche. The last is my addition, as is this conclusion: the Great Mother is God.

A Summing Up

The answer seems plain now, after years of reading, thinking, and writing: our egos arise from the Great Mother, from the unconscious pool into which we are born, and we leave this wetly warm state of yin for the perilous, cold state of yang. The conscious, creative yang of the ego is a decades-long period of absorbing experiences and distilling them into a set of values. Then, usually at the age when the active ego begins to rest, around sixty years, the option arises: go back to the warmly wet yin of infancy, or enter the unknown yang of inner experiences.

The yin state is characterized by retirement homes where the clacking of false teeth makes more impression than new ideas. The usual progression here is fairly steep, ending in the grave, or a vegetal state equivalent to it. For those who consciously choose the yang state, and who move felicitously from the macrocosm to the microcosm, there is a growing feeling of intense creativity, heralded by a frequent glimpse of the answer to man's search for meaning. The ego's triumphs of the macrocosm come to mind, but they pale by comparison with these later microcosmic ones.

Two of the great minds of the past hundred years, Arnold Toynbee and Carl Jung, have agreed with this thesis as evidenced by the spiritual biographies each of them wrote at the end of his life. "Everything transitory is only approximation; what could not be achieved, here comes to pass; what no one could describe is here accomplished; womanhood everlasting (the Great Mother) draws us aloft" (Goethe's *Faust*). These are the last words sung in both Liszt's *A Faust Symphony*, and in Mahler's *Eighth Symphony*.

Chapter Twenty-One
The Origins and History of
Consciousness

In this book, Neumann focuses on how the human consciousness progresses through archetypical stages and how myth influences that progression. In the first part, he discusses the creation myth, the hero myth, and then transformation myths.

He says that in the beginning, the world and the unconscious predominated. Man's arrival at consciousness, or when light comes into the world, is the basis of the creation myth. As the World Parents are separated, ego consciousness is born and the hero myth begins. This creation is seen both as the creation of man as well as, individually, the earliest dawn of childhood.

During my doctoral research in the early 1970s in East Africa, all of my interviewees told me the same story about the creation, namely that their families went back in an unbroken string to the first man, who, instead of being a mythical Adam, was a mythical Jesus Christ. This progenitor could be dated, by generations, to around AD 1570, and bore little resemblance to either the historical figure or the religious one. These peoples, mainly from the west and northwest of

Kenya and the northeast of Uganda, had first encountered Christianity some sixty years before when the first missionaries arrived around 1910. They had accepted Christ enthusiastically into their own religion and history, much as the earlier Germans had also accepted Christianity because of Christ's similarity to their own God.

Neumann concludes that consciousness is the object of creative mythology. The Creation is also our first question: where did we come from? More particularly, where did I come from? This is why Genesis is both so long an introduction to the Bible, and also so important.

The only other question of equal import is our search for meaning, which includes the creation; both of these are what Neumann wrote his book(s) about, and they concern me as deeply as they did him; hence, I am writing about Neumann's book, but really about life itself, as evidenced in all the books quoted in this one.

The reason Erich Neumann, Carl Jung, Arnold Toynbee, and others write is partially to enable others to read their thinking, but largely to help the writer better understand their own thinking. It is a creative process, meaning that the writer gathers their references together to illustrate their points, necessitating a rereading of these references, and this is where those references become creative.

For example, I often refer to JJ Bachofen in my writing but usually quote him from memory rather than rereading his original words. Last year, I added a chapter on him to my recent book (*Out of Kenya* 2005), which necessitated the rereading of his *Myth, Religion and Mother Right* for the first time in some twenty years. Amazing how writers we think we know well change, apparently, in a decade or two; of course, it's us who change, as we mature and modify our thoughts and add new ideas to the mix.

My academic mentor, Roy P. Fairfield, wrote recently to describe his latest writing, about the one hundred books most influential on his thinking, just as I was writing this book about the ten or so writers that have most heavily influenced my life. Then I read Harold Bloom's recent (2004) *Where Shall Wisdom Be Found?*, a book about the dozen or so writers he admires most. An intriguing book, as Bloom's books tend to be, but quite different from either Roy Fairfield's or my books on the same subject.

However, Bloom's book stirred me deeply as I argued with his choices and conclusions, which is what books are also written for. Then I read Bloom's later book *Jesus and Yahweh: The Names Divine*, written in 2005, and simply enjoyed myself, especially when Bloom suggested what for him was a typical comparison, which I paraphrase as: God is to Jesus as King Lear is to Hamlet. This is such a different approach to all four of these personalities that I began annoying my friends with the idea, which is one thing friends are for.

The main idea here is our changing of perceptions rather than the people or ideas themselves changing.

Returning to Neumann and creation, we see that from creation comes the symbol, an analogy and therefore containing a wealth of meanings, but also elusive. Neumann says that only symbols can "make something unknown, and beyond the grasp of consciousness, more intelligible and more capable of becoming conscious" (*The Origins and History of Consciousness*).

The first symbol is the round, the sphere, the circle, the egg, the "self-contained," without beginning or end, also the container of opposites. This symbol is also the World Parents, or heaven and earth before they split. Neumann defines this state before the light of creation as the Uroboros, or snake biting its tail and thereby forming a circle which represents a container: the maternal womb and also masculine and feminine opposites, or World Parents.

Adam and Eve existed in the Uroboros, also known as the Garden of Eden, the sphere of preconsciousness, from which they could only escape through the help of the uroboric snake. Neumann says this Edenic garden was never a historical state. Leaving the Garden, sometimes misnamed Paradise, is going from yin to yang, from the unconscious to the conscious.

This is the real creation, the dawn of the first light, the first stirrings of ego consciousness, and we'll never know when it happened because there would need to have been a conscious ego there to record its own birth. One of the first conscious egos described the creation of man as the Breath of God, a metaphor I admire because it's close to my own concept of God as human.

The Great Mother The Ego under the Dominance of the Uroboros

When the ego severs its own umbilical cord from the uroboros, it becomes aware of the qualities of pleasure and pain. As mentioned earlier, the bad mother and the good mother are two sides of the Great Mother, who is in charge of this stage, indicating we are in the matriarchal period. As consciousness develops, the matriarchy weakens to the point where the patriarchy takes over. The early years of the patriarchy now become the later matriarchy years.

Orestes and Oedipus follow in the line of "heroes" who change the matriarchy into patriarchy. This adolescent stage of the ego is just an emergence into maturity, where it will become independent of the unconscious. Oedipus symbolizes this late adolescent stage as he is overwhelmed by fate, and yet he suggests emerging into a more mature world through the aid of Antigone. At least he ends his life in hope instead of despair.

Representative of this emergence of the mature ego is Orestes, for he is devoted to his father, Agamemnon, as is his sister, Elektra. As Neumann puts it: "In the *Oresteia* the son stands squarely on the side of the father. Liberation from the mother has gone even further ... in the *Oresteia* and again with variations in *Hamlet*, the spirit of the father is the impelling force that compasses the death of the sinful mother."

Here, identification with the father is so complete that the maternal principle is stifled even when it appears, not in the symbolic form of a dragon, but as the real mother, and she is killed precisely because this principle has sinned against the father principle.

The Separation of the World Parents: The Principle of Opposites

Next, Neumann talks about the separation of the World Parents. Returning to the Creation, the circle, the egg, or uroboros, heaven and earth were joined to make the whole, the father representing heaven above and the mother the earth below. The "creation" of light thereby separates the World Parents and makes consciousness possible. The same light illuminated the Garden of Eden and brought those world parents to life outside it, much as Prometheus brought the light of fire to Man, creating human consciousness as it destroyed the old gods in the process.

Ego consciousness is represented by many historical events, as disparate as Turkey's great humanist poet Yunus Emre's writing in the twelfth century, and Michelangelo's painting in the sixteenth century. The Renaissance, or *Rinascimento* in Italian, is the celebration of the maturity of the individual ego in consciousness.

By this same criterion, the civilization of the East is typified by the submergence of the individual to society, and therefore represents a less mature ego consciousness. Ego consciousness is Pandora's Box, it is escape from the Garden of Eden, it is the Renaissance, the flowering of Western civilization and its concomitant Götterdämmerung.

According to Neumann, escaping the Terrible Mother and becoming a conscious ego requires several steps or battles. Once the ego emerges, however, it adopts the tactics of the Terrible Mother, represented in mythology by the slaying of the dragon, for instance by my namesake. Therefore, George, or Saint George, is a symbol of the formation of the conscious ego of the hero, and to the raising of the treasure: knowledge.

Wagner's Siegfried illustrates this theme by tasting the dragon's blood after he slays it, and thereby understands the language of the birds.

The Hero Myth

Neumann's next section is about the hero myth, where he discusses the birth of the hero and the slaying of the father and mother. He writes about the hero, or the "hero stage" that all of us go through. Despite having multiple parents, the essence of the hero is that he is an "apparent" orphan, or else has divine parentage, such as Wagner's Siegfried, who had both.

In order for us of the third millennium after Christ to understand the meaning of these myths, we must agree with Neumann that the word "virginity" simply means not belonging to any man, or a state of openness to God. It is almost impossible to comprehend the meaning of virgin or virgin birth or numinous parentage from the patriarchal viewpoint. The real "miracle" is that a woman is able to produce a male from within herself.

All primitive cultures ascribed this activity to gods, or winds or holy spirits, before sexual union was recognized as the origin.

The Slaying of the Mother

Once born, the hero stands between the separated World Parents and he challenges them to fight him in what all cultures refer to as a dragon-fight. Firenze has almost as many representations of Saint George killing the dragon as they have Last Suppers, usually showing all three elements necessary to this myth: dragon, hero, and treasure. The treasure is usually a naked virgin, but as Wagner illustrates in Siegfried, it can also include magic helmets, cloaks, and rings.

The hero is exemplified by Siegfried: immature, dumb, groping for meaning, devoid of fear. This is the newly conscious ego struggling to break free of the unconscious, the uroboros. And the uroboros is represented by the dragon, both male and female. Neumann quotes Jung to show that they agree on this important point: the hero's dragon-fight is essentially with the mother, but not her personally; it is with the mother archetype.

The second point that Neumann and Jung agree upon is that victory over the mother frequently involves actual coition with her, or incest, which is a regenerative incest that brings about a rebirth. Neumann becomes weak here, and cites Jung to strengthen his case: "For the ego and the male, the female is synonymous with the unconscious and the nonego, hence with darkness, nothingness, the void, the bottomless pit."

Both Neumann and Jung go too far in this chapter, equating "mother, the womb, the pit and hell." What has happened, been written about, discussed and helped to express our present culture during the fifty years since Neumann and Jung last wrote, changes their position about women and woman. For example, I don't believe either Jung or Neumann could fathom the 1994 lawsuit for discrimination in Chicago against a professor for using a biblical anecdote to illustrate his teaching.

The story, which the professor had been using for thirty years, is about the man who accidentally fell off his roof onto a woman, with whom he then copulated. His point was that the man could not be accused of rape because it was an accident. The female student who sued claimed that it was a sexist story. If I were the professor, I would change the story, not delete it: the carpenter on the roof should become a female and fiddle the poor fellow she fell upon.

Neumann cites a good example, of Samson yielding to Delilah, the Great Mother, who castrates him by cutting his hair and blinding him. Samson's triumph, and sacrificial death, restore Jehovah, the patriarchy personified.

An even older tale is next told, of the symbolic swallowing of the sun each evening by the sea dragon. He is reborn each morning as the *sol invictus*, his victorious rebirth an affirmation of patriarchal power.

On an annual basis, Christ represents the patriarchal principle, born at the darkest point of the year as light. To me, this patriarchal concept is as fundamental as Orestes' slaying of his mother to illustrate the change from matriarchy to patriarchy.

The Slaying of the Father

The "father" discussed here is both negative and positive, creative and destructive, just as the "mother" is. The mother, however, represents instinct, eternal and almost unalterable. Neumann next puts his finger on the real difference between these World Parents, writing that paternal authority differs from maternal authority in that it is relative, whereas maternal authority is absolute.

Before the current speedup of change, it was only the hero who challenged the old system, making him a "breaker of the old law." This hero also is usually born of a virgin through a god who engenders the new order. For this reason, the hero is frequently abandoned or exposed at birth, although there is usually a prophecy that the son will take over the kingdom from his father. Examples are rife, from Hercules to Oedipus to Jesus, but the important thing is that their lives form a concatenation of events that exemplify the hero who destroys the old as he brings on the new. Neumann concludes that the conflict between the hero and the father is not personal but transpersonal: what the hero transforms, transforms him.

The Captive and the Treasure

The goal of the dragon-fight is usually the naked virgin waiting to reward St. George; she is otherwise known as the "Captive." Neumann suggests that the Wagnerian gold in his *Ring Cycle* is both a late and degenerate form of the original treasure motif. The duality of the above suggests that it operates in differing ways for different humans. Therefore, there is an actual naked virgin waiting to be freed, which represents St. George's soul, also waiting to breathe free.

In order for the soul, or ego-consciousness, to break free, the "dragon" must be killed, and it is the Great Mother, in particular the Terrible Mother aspect of her, that must be overthrown and destroyed. Once the Great Mother is overthrown, the hero can claim the captive, the maiden, and the treasure, or perhaps all three in one.

But wait, the maiden is not a simple virgin waiting to escape the Terrible Mother dragon, for she also has needs, vast ones, from escaping magical powers to overcoming joyless depression. He who thinks to take the easy way out and avoid confrontation with the Terrible Mother must live with that Terrible Mother dominating him forever, a fate otherwise known as alienation.

Neumann writes that the captive is the treasure or somehow related to it. Wagner's Siegfried killed his dragon, but when he tried to rescue the maiden, Brunnhilda, she proved far too much woman for him. He failed in that relationship because of his immaturity, and died from that very failure, although he had the "treasure" in his grasp. This "treasure" is more than a woman, or a mate, or even anything material; the treasure is contained within the rite of passage, i.e., the killing of the dragon, but the culture-hero must realize it is also the "water of life, immortality, fertility and the after-life rolled into one" (*The Great Mother*).

This, Siegfried was incapable of doing. Further, achieving this point, this understanding, is a "genuine creation, and the symbolic recitation of the story of creation at the new year has its rightful place at this point." Neumann writes that it is impossible to find this treasure, meaning the inner knowledge that Siegfried never achieved, unless the hero "has first found and redeemed his own soul, his own feminine counterpart which conceived and brings forth" (*The Great Mother*).

Siegfried failed this test we all must face, just as Christ succeeded, according to me.

I find an example of this in my own life. I confronted my own Terrible Mother in the person of my maternal grandmother. We conceived a dislike for each other based on my unwillingness to bow before her might. My mother did bow before her mother's demands, but I alone fought the old dragon and symbolically slew her, in court, and then, adding incest to insult to injury, I took over her power, the newspaper she controlled, and wrote my own story of Creation from this treasure.

Transformation, or Osiris

This is the final section about transformation myths. Neumann defines three types of hero: the introvert, the extrovert, and the centrovert. What he misses in his analysis is that most people go through these stages in the ordinary course of life, and some times are in at least two stages at the same time, and may be there for many years. I was conscious that my centroversion stage began in 1991 when I consciously gave up my exhilarating forty-three-year career in journalism just after my exciting but enervating eighteen months on the Berlin Wall and in Eastern Europe, ending up in Soviet Russia. I deliberately forsook those glories, those louse-infested beds, bad meals, and worse wine, and traded it all in for the life of introversion and centroversion. I stopped writing journalistically and began writing these books.

I left the world of the macrocosm for the life of the microcosm. I ceased doing and began being. I stopped living outside and started investigating my mind. I did not turn from yang to yin; I have found even more yangness inside than I ever encountered outside. I believe that this is the true transformation, or centroversion, or individuation, but it's still in progress, inshallah.

One of the basic phenomena of all initiation rites is that the ancestor is reincarnated in the initiate. This can be traced historically from Osiris through Christ to our own individuation. This is what I think Jesus meant when he said, "I and the Father are one." Or, Osiris and Horus are one, just as Demeter and Persephone are one as are Psyche and Aphrodite.

The Psychological Stages in the Development of Personality: The Original Unity

The second part of Neumann's book focuses on the original unity, the separation of the systems, the balance and crisis of consciousness, and centroversion and stages of life.

Neumann says that the purpose of his book is to show the importance of myth for our Western civilization, and to show how it has assisted the growth of the individual personality. For example, the structure of Goethe's *Faust* looks at Faust's characteristics and activities, whereas genetically we look at Faust as part of Goethe's personality.

Neumann comments on centroversion in organisms on the uroboric level, saying that centroversion is the innate tendency of an individual in order to create unity. Thus the first stirrings of consciousness and the ego. But the ego relates in a different way to the body because it represents a higher principle, according to Neumann, working through the head and consciousness.

An example is the image-symbol "fire." It is seen as red, or burning, representing both inner and outer experiences combining to form the ego's reaction to these experiences. When these images are instinctual they are what Jung termed archetypes. Neumann doesn't specifically say it, but each of us human beings is obviously capable of being a hero. To qualify that assertion: each ordinary human has that capability; only those who never emerge from the clutches of the Great Mother do not become heroes.

We have now gone from the familiar chaos of creation to visible forms, and these forms tend to develop from the theriomorphic to the anthropomorphic, from animal form to possessing human characteristics. The ego is assertive in its new consciousness. Neumann does not carry his imagery forward to this area of higher consciousness, but it's obvious that the progression from the formlessness of chaos through the theriomorphic to the anthropomorphic culminates in the abstract, since that is what the higher consciousness can now both conceive and be.

Arnold Toynbee had reflections in a similar vein; after proceeding from the macrocosm of the emerging ego to the microcosm of the inner self, his image of God progressed from the anthropomorphic to the abstract: Deus est mortale iuvare mortalem.

Centroversion and Differentiation

Neumann goes deeply into this situation, concluding that the conscious ego can exert a great influence for itself on the unconscious. I noticed this strong instinct in myself at an early age, and also learned to use it to resolve personal situations.

It required years to realize that an upsurge of my feelings always calls forth a like upsurge in others. From this simple action-reaction process I learned that if I could control my own feelings, then my chances of success in an encounter were greatly improved.

There's an alternative which is even better, as illustrated by my Florentine friend Ronaldo. Recently, he was tapped from behind by another car. Normally, this means a cessation of traffic while everyone gets out to witness how the two principals will settle this matter of honor. Rolando walked back to the other Italian, kissed him on both cheeks, and drove away, leaving a stupefied fellow standing in the road.

Maybe nature doesn't favor the individual, but I do, and so does Rolando; and individuals who exert their minds to control their instincts will usually win in a battle with the collective. To reconstruct, it is only when the hero slays the dragon, or the Great Mother, that he frees the princess, his anima, and makes her his partner and becomes whole, as once the Father and Mother were.

Another way of looking at this scene is that the princess, or treasure or anima, is in the power of the dragon, or Great Mother, which "distorts her and her humanity," and it is this distortion that must be overcome. This is the mythical and fairy-tale theme of disenchantment, as seen by Sleeping Beauty being awakened by the prince's kiss.

Neumann next stresses a point that I consider crucial, and yet one that Jung almost doesn't mention; namely, that the anima and the animus are equal and equally important to both man and to woman, and whenever he uses the term "anima" it is mutatis mutandis the "animus."

The Balance and Crisis of Consciousness

Recently I told a story to a group in Firenze; I related to them Apulieus's version of the myth of Amor and Psyche, which I retitled Aphrodite and Psyche, taking fifteen minutes to sketch the first half of the story. I became fascinated by the reaction of my sophisticated group: they were fascinated! This primordial myth spoke to them with a "thousand voices" and precipitated a very lively discussion. It raises a real question: why don't church preachers, with such a wealth of primordial myth at hand in the Bible and Koran, use these myths in their sermons? Why do they instead stifle their parishioners' intellects while they still their emotions with desert-dry personal evaluations of what they think the Bible means?

I believe that the above is the real reason for the present rise of fundamentalism in all the world's religions: these fundamentalists at least know how to stir the emotions of their flocks, and they are good at throwing primordial images, distorted and out of context though they may be, at their people.

Neumann describes change in the twentieth century and what the quickening of the amount of change means to us. Although change involves both movement and countermovement, it is moving from unconsciousness to consciousness. This both agrees and contrasts with Arnold Toynbee's analysis of change, which was made at about the same time as Neumann's.

It does make us wonder, now in 2007, what difference the enormous speed-up in change would have made to thinkers like Neumann and Jung if they lived through such change as we have witnessed since both of them died. I bought my first computer in 1962, about the time those two were at the end of their lives, and that Control Data monster could only hyphenate and justify lines of type. This iBook I'm typing on today is less than a hundredth the size of the first computer I bought, but I cannot even try to quantify the difference in what the two machines can do. Each month some new marvel comes out for computers that I feel I must buy in order to keep up.

And I used to keep a camera for years, slowly acquiring the full use of it, whereas my digital camera today needs replacing every year. I think that the pace of change is challenging our minds to stretch and grow just to keep up, and therefore the process is a good one. The price keeps decreasing, making the technology affordable to more and more people. This process is working to make great changes in almost all our lives in this world, and despite the unfortunate but necessary changes in the working places that make for unemployment somewhere while creating jobs elsewhere, having a temporarily disastrous effect on some, the overall effect is good, especially for the third world as it struggles to rise up to the first.

I would like to discuss the above with Neumann because it appears that my concept of God falls under his interdiction, but I believe that the two of us could explain our differing interpretations satisfactorily to each other. There is ample room for transpersonal and archetypal interpretations in "Deus est mortale iuvare mortalem." The above was written over fifty years ago, and today in 2007, civilization demonstrates the aptness of Neumann's words anew. But he concludes this chapter about a culture in crisis in an upbeat way, saying that the future can be saved, but only by the hero, or the individual.

Centroversion and the Stages of Life

Neumann claims that the first half of life is marked by two fights with the dragon, and I agree that the first encounter is before age seven, or the age of reason, and the second at puberty, or twice the first age. He ends this book some fifty pages later without suggesting there are other, continuing, dragon-fights that last throughout life. Each encounter with the Earth Mother leaves us stronger and better—equipped to meet the next challenge. If one accepts Neumann's first two age groupings, roughly seven and fourteen, I suggest that a continuance of the seven-year span is fairly accurate. For example, as much change as occurs within an individual from birth to age seven, and again at puberty, there is as much more change by the age of twenty-one, and again at twenty-eight, and so on.

When we stop changing every seven years or so, we have begun to decay and die. Think of all the changes you have gone through during life, and there is an interesting grouping of times, of "dragon-fights" that precipitate change. And is this not a principle of life we have found? I believe that Neumann and Jung thought so.

I describe the principle thus: in order to grow, each of us must keep killing the dragon on a fairly regular basis throughout life, although we never destroy the dragon on a personal level until we die, for the dragon, of course, is within us, and may be us. As Pogo famously reminded us in his comic strip: "We have met the enemy and he is us." The reason for this is that, like freedom or other basic human rights, we are dealing with primordial human nature, which cannot change because it is archetypal and, hence, immortal.

Chapter Twenty-Two
Myth, Religion, and Mother Right

The closing chapter of this book assumes the reader has read my 2005 book, published in England by Book Guild Publishing: *Out of Kenya, Out of Istanbul*, especially the last chapter based on Johann J. Bachofen and his great book *Myth, Religion and Mother Right*.

JJ Bachofen (1815–87) is one of a trio of oft-quoted masters I have come to know by footnote for many decades. The other two are usually connected with their best-known works, Frazer's *The Golden Bough* and Apuleius' *The Golden Ass*, both of which are good books to read and also great references. But Bachofen's essays in his *Myth, Religion and Mother Right* are more than that: they are seminal, like Picasso's paintings.

This reflection on Bachofen is from the last chapter of my recent (2005) book *Out of Kenya, Out of Istanbul*, rewritten here because of its importance to my reading and writing and life itself. In my copy of Bachofen's book, Joseph Campbell writes the introduction and quotes Bachofen writing to his mentor, Karl von Savigny, that he feels he is close to his goal of finding "the eternal footprint," or the law that governs all things, the Holy Grail we all search for.

As an example, Campbell uses the myth of Sisyphus, condemned by Zeus to roll his rock up the hill every day, as the representative of life itself, the eternal partner of death. As the rock rolls back to the valley at the end of each day, Sisyphus is free of his burden and becomes the symbol of hope and hence of life.

Albert Camus suggested in his book on Sisyphus that this period of walking downhill symbolized mankind's rest period at the end of a day of useless labor. I think that it represents more than individual man's striving for rest, or even for creativity. It's the symbol of life just as much as rolling the rock uphill symbolizes death, or despair.

But Sisyphus is also a world-class trickster, like Odysseus, or Hermes and Iris, and hence he represents hope in an apparently hopeless situation.

Bachofen points out that the oldest symbols of mankind are from tombs, and depict the wheel going around and returning to its starting point much as Sisyphus does, or the snake consuming itself as in Mayan depictions, which Neumann called the "uroboros." He writes that all ancient religions began with this concept of progressing to the beginning; the cycle of life and death that has intrigued mankind since the first mind could apprehend it.

Yet, as Arnold Toynbee concluded, history is not static, but dynamic, and changes for the better over the long run. The Dionysian religion exemplified this fact, and the Eleusinian Mysteries contained it as their central mystery. Yet Bachofen was not perfect, nor as close to it as the other authors I have written about above. He lived and wrote before the others did, and lacked their input into his thinking as well as all the wonders the last century has brought to us through technology. I consider chief among these to be the speed at which we can now write, beginning with the pencil and paper that we share with Bachofen, but progressing ever more quickly to typewriters and electric typewriters through all those other machines to the present computers and their keyboards that can keep up with the speed of mind, a vital function for all writers from journalists to nuclear physicists.

Bachofen demonstrates his lack of agreement with me by writing a chapter on Amor and Psyche that insults most of my thinking, reading, and writing on the subject.. He suggests that the moon is hermaphroditic because it's a union of two principles: mother and virgin, which he incorrectly calls Amor and Psyche; if he had had access to Erich Neumann's writings on this subject he would have developed his theme using Demeter and Persephone instead. This concept was developed over fifty years after Bachofen wrote, so his thinking helped to form the basis for Jung's and Kerenyi's writings, especially their conclusion that Demeter and Persephone were one.

Bachofen wrote that myth precedes history and therefore it also contains origins. He concludes this thought by stating that myth is bound up with the earliest religions, especially those under the ancient matriarchies.

Bachofen's central thesis is that the earliest matriarchies needed to conflict with, and be surpassed by, the Demetrian principle in order to prepare the way for the eventually dominant patriarchal principle to come into its hegemony. Let's accept this thesis as an assumption and view it historically through Toynbee's long-distance lens. The implication is that our present patriarchy is but step three in humankind's march to maturity and consciousness. We are merely at our teenage, or heroic, or epic, level, with the best yet to come.

At this point Bachofen writes that reaching this point in the progress from a maternal to a paternal conception of humanity is the "most important turning point." I have thought about this moment in history and wondered if it occurred because people recognized that the male sperm was responsible for fertilizing the female egg.

Nobody has seriously answered this question, but it is both logical and rational. By definition this is impossible to prove, much as it is impossible to know exactly what were the Eleusinian Mysteries, but we have amassed a far more historical record going back to this prehistorical time than Bachofen thought that we could.

Recently, for example, the wonderful cave paintings near Avignon in France have illuminated the prehistorical culture with historical data, and, incidentally, sent those pictures around the computer-connected world. Bachofen sees this historic moment of passage from matriarchy to patriarchy exemplified by Orestes avenging his father's death by killing his mother.

The old law is set by the Furies, wherein Orestes' guilt is basically inexpiable despite the justice, apparent to our Western, patriarchal senses, of avenging his mother's murder of his father. The new law, that of the higher patriarchy, is ushered in by both Athena and Apollo. This also implies that the mother's divinity now passes to the father. The matriarchy is characterized by the unconscious, the patriarchy by the conscious.

Toynbee would say that the pendulum swings from the East, where society dominates the individual, to the West, where the individual dominates society. The Immortal is no longer the earth and the female, but the heaven-sent male who now rules the earth. Bachofen quotes the Bible to illustrate: "For man is not of woman, but woman is of the man."

Both Jung and Neumann described this change from matriarchy to patriarchy as "individuation." Bachofen asserts that Aeschylus described the transfer of matriarchy to patriarchy in his *Oresteia* because Orestes' trial was won by patriarchy over matriarchy. It was Apollo's deed that accomplished this sea-change in human affairs, and he was aided by Zeus' non-matriarchal daughter Athena.

Bachofen concludes his monumental book by adding the *Oedipodeia* to his quotes on the *Oresteia*, thus thrusting Oedipus' troubles on to a new stage, a new influence on our lives as we accumulate evidence of the fundamental shift from mother to father. To me, the tragedy of Oedipus is more meaningful to my life than Orestes' struggles, and I feel that Oedipus' final hours with his daughter Antigone are some of the finest lines in dramatic history, illuminating one of the great ideas in life.

Reference List

Gibran, Kahlil. Milano, Italy, 1993. *The Prophet.*

Fowles, John. *Daniel Martin.*

Toynbee, Arnold. *A Study of History, 12 vols*

Toynbee, Arnold. *Experiences.*OUP,

Toynbee, Arnold: *An historian's Approach to Religion*

Campbell, Joseph. *Creative Mythology.*

Campbell, Joseph. *The Hero With 1,000 Faces.*

Campbell, Joseph. *The Masks of God*

Campbell, Joseph. *Occidental Mythology.*

Campbell, Joseph. *Myths to Live By.*

Jung, Carl. articles on mythology

Neumann, Erich. *Eros & Psyche.*

Neumann, Erich. *The Great Mother.*

Neumann, Erich. *The Origins and History of Consciousness.*

Kerenyi, Karl. *Archetypal Image of Eleusis*

Kerenyi, Karl. and Jung, Carl. *Essays on a Science of Mythology.*

Bachofen, Johann J. *Myth, Religion, and Mother Right.*

Palladio. Andrea. *The Four Books of Architecture.*

Conrad, Joseph. *Lord Jim*

Lawrence, David Herbert. *The Rainbow.*

Fitzgerald, F. Scott. *This Side of Paradise.*

Lessing, Doris. *The Summer Before the Dark*

Dostoevsky, Fyodor. "The Grand Inquisitor." *The Brothers Karamazov.*

Kuser, George. *Out of Kenya, Out of Istanbul/UK/The Book Guild/2005*

Richter, Conrad. *The Trees.*

Richter, Conrad. *The Fields.*

Richter, Conrad. *The Town.*

Alinsky, Saul. *Reveille for Radicals/Rules for Radicals*

Bloom, Harold. *Shakespeare, The Invention of the Human*

Bloom, Harold. *Jesus and Yahweh: the Names Divine*

Bloom, Harold. *Where Shall Wisdom be Found?*

Armstrong, Karen. *The Spiral Staircase.*

Armstrong, Karen. *The Great Transformation.*

Goldstein, Rebecca. *Betraying Spinoza.*

Sebastian de Grazia. *Machiavelli in Hell*

Camus, Albert. *Sisyphus/UK/Penguin/1955*

Frankl, Viktor. *Man's Search for Meaning*

Auel, Jean: *The Clan of the Cave Bear* (5 volumes)/UK/Hoddard Stoughton/2002

Virgil. *The Aeneid.* trans. by Robert Fagles, 2006

Von Goethe, Johann W. *Faust*

Paralipomenon

I conclude this book with a narrative bibliography and an introduction to people who have been as influential on my life and thinking as the writers I've written about. I believe this will add up to a coherent picture of one person's approach to maturity through reading and thinking.

The books I wrote about are each mentioned in order in the Reference List, and they are buttressed by all the hundreds of others that I wandered through, or studied, during my life. I studied anthropology at the University of Nairobi, but I was never an anthropologist. My academic mentor, Dr. Roy P. Fairfield, guided me through the depths of a PhD, but I tended to wander through the shallows, becoming fascinated by the Kenyan tribes and individuals I worked with, often spending days talking with people who had oral knowledge only, supplying my actual research with little, but enriching my personal life enormously. I think of myself as a professional amateur, carefully avoiding becoming an amateur professional. My reading has been like that all my life, leading me into strange paths that do not count toward a PhD but have made my life interesting.

People, Extraneous but Important to Me

I enjoy speaking with specialists, such as historians, for they tend to sense a thread of continuity about life, but so many specialists spend most of their time reading within their specialty that they miss the pleasures of knowing great minds outside their field.

I attended the Lawrenceville School for six years, and that experience meant as much as anything else I've done, for it opened my mind, between the ages of eleven and seventeen, to such authors as Rudyard Kipling and Charles Dickens, and I read poetry for the first time, catching the cadences in my mind forever. Macaulay's epic poem "Horatio at the Bridge" is probably not very good poetry, but for a teenager in the heroic stage of life it sings a siren song that stirs me still.

My first math teacher, Frederici by name, introduced me to dull numbers brightly through encouraging us to multiply, in our minds only, three numbers by another three numbers, like 362 times 848, and feel elated by the ease of it. I have no further education in mathematics, but that first teacher awakened me to such wonderful possibilities of what my mind could do, especially when I wait in a teller's line at my bank and watch people miscount simple numbers because they lack the gifted teacher that I had.

As I mention in my last book, the reason I went to East Africa to live and work was primarily Karen Blixen's books, but I was captured by Africa years before that, while Karen was still in Kenya, by the Tarzan books that set my mind on fire to see his jungles and his apes. Bomba The Jungle Boy came even earlier, and perhaps I would be in Africa yet if it weren't for my family and business bringing me back to reality.

Rather than list those books that formed my mind and character, I want to tell you about one writer who opened my mind as well as my heart, yet is little-known today. Conrad Richter moved from Pennsylvania to Ohio decades after the families he wrote so movingly about, but he managed to meet and talk with some of the pioneers and their descendants, and was able to empathize with them and their struggles.

He picked up the idiosyncratic speech those pioneers spoke, and wrote so well about their struggles that we, the readers, identify with their individual needs, troubles, and lives. Following largely one family through the years of struggle is a wonderful experience for anyone who lives in Ohio today. For me, having just moved to Ohio from New Jersey, it was an introduction to the living history of the area I worked and lived in for twelve years.

Richter wrote three books, finally published in one large one called *The Trees, The Fields, The Town*, and I highly recommend all three to anybody, but especially to people residing in those parts of the United States that were settled by pioneers; in other words, the whole country. A lot of my friends are academics or specialists, and they devote their reading lives to their specialty. However, Conrad Richter's books are something many of those specialists miss, and I believe that their lives are narrowed by missing his writing. Enjoy.

J. Montgomery Curtis

I have worked with journalists all my life, but the guy who interested me most, and who influenced my life in journalism most, is J. Montgomery Curtis. He was a generation older than I, so he was at the top as I began closer to the bottom. We met when he came to Columbia University as the head of the American Press Institute, a school for professional journalists, and he made his imprint on me almost the day he started. Monty was alive with knowledge of journalism, as well as knowing many of the journalists around the world, and he helped design courses to attract the best and to help them learn about each other and how to make better newspapers.

When I won a long court case and took over management of the *Trenton Times*, Monty became a member of our family-dominated board of directors. That was in 1961, and Monty is the only person I know who could have handled some of my screwball relatives and allowed me to manage the paper. At one time, near the end of his career in journalism, I asked why he was only on two newspaper boards. He replied: "Because only two ever asked me."

Shortly after that, he left Columbia University to work full-time for the Knight-Ridder newspaper group and be on their board as well. His job was a dream fulfilled at that stage of his life, for he moved to Miami, using the *Miami Herald* as his base office, and traveled throughout America, talking with other Knight-Ridder newspapers about improving their news product.

I visited Monty in Miami shortly after he moved there, and he proudly showed off his lovely home, and then had a small dinner to introduce me to the two Knight brothers, John and Jim, and we all talked shop deep into the night. Monty told me about discovering that the small island he now lived on was a "restricted" island, meaning no Jews were allowed. Monty had to inform the Knight brothers that he was Jewish, and their reply was to laugh as they told him he was also now a member of their local country club, which was equally restricted. The three of them thought it a joke, and it was amusing, but it also was a correction of an outrageous insult.

Besides attending many sessions at Columbia run by Monty, I became interested in his summer project involving bringing foreign editors to America to attend sessions at Columbia and then travel around the United States. The program was funded by the Ford Foundation, and Monty asked me to spend several months touring Scandinavia and selecting twenty or so journalists to participate in the next year's program. That was one of the best ideas I ever worked through, especially with Monty's expert guidance. The conclusion, for me, was meeting the participants in New York, and working with them for a month or so, then helping them with their itineraries. Their school days at Columbia ended in August, just before Labor Day, and I had a company plane I was flying to Ohio to be with my family over the holidays, so six of the Scandinavians agreed to start their U.S. travels with five days at my home in Ohio.

I know they enjoyed seeing American life via those days in a small Ohio town after a month in New York City, and I know my Ohio town reciprocated the enjoyment and the chance to meet these wonderful people.

Another time with Monty came shortly before he retired, while I was the head of a large group of newspapers headquartered in Chicago. We held a meeting for a thousand of our editors and publishers, and I invited Monty to be guest speaker, asking him to send me the biographical material I could use to introduce him. I was amazed at the amount he sent me, and an idea popped into my head, which resulted in my rising at the end of the dinner with the thousand journalists, clutching a large number of papers as I looked at Monty sitting nearby, knowing that he expected me to spend maybe ten minutes introducing him.

Instead, "Our speaker today needs no introduction," I said, and sat down.

Monty took his glasses off, wiping the tears of laughter from his eyes, as he embraced me before making his speech. When Monty died, a part of me did, too.

Ellen Stewart, La Mama

Ellen Stewart is an All-American genius, but she is better recognized elsewhere in the world than she is in America, except for in New York City, where she is an icon of the theater world. I have written more articles about her than I can recall, and produced plays for her and with her in many parts of the world, but when I thought of getting together the definitive book of her life in theater, it quickly became obvious that it would take somebody with at least two years to dedicate to the research, and loads of money to pay for the travel around the world.

I discussed it with Ellen, of course, and she had in mind a large book with lots of pictures. This was maybe fifteen years ago, in the early 1990s, and there were two sources to start with: the La Mama archives in New York, organized by my old friend Ozzie Rodriguez, and the international archives, in Rome, organized by Claudia Ruspoli.

I discussed the book with each of them, and we agreed that what they had in their separate archives was essential, but less than half of what existed. The job looked, and still appears to be, enormous, although the money should be relatively easy to arrange with a book publisher in combination with some of the foundations that have supported La Mama so generously over the years. Well, Ellen is nearing her fiftieth anniversary in theater, and we don't seem to be getting closer to the actual book, but I think it is essential we do something to at least start organizing for it because so much of the material exists most excitingly through recollections by living people, mainly Ellen herself.

I have an ongoing file on Ellen Stewart here at my home in Italy, less than a kilometer from her La Mama Umbria property for artists-in-residence and performance spaces, and that file has bulged out into two more files, so when I think about her many stories haunt my mind. If I summed them all up, however, one of Ellen's greatest attributes is her personal loyalty to her people all over the world a side of her that she has shown me frequently.

I was spending the summer at my Aegean Sea home in Assos, just south of ancient Troy, in 1992, and I received a phone call telling me my mother died, full of good times and years. Everybody expected me to return to the United States for the funeral, but my mother and I had often discussed death, and our agreement was it should not be celebrated publicly. I told my family I would stay in Assos and grieve privately.

Then Ellen called and said she was coming to stay with me for several days. This not only involved her flying to Istanbul, but driving for five hours from there. The next day she arrived, and we sat and talked for a couple of days about life and death. Her conclusion was that I was not an orphan, but now I was really her son. Since those days in Assos, La Mama and I have argued, fought, and spent months not speaking to each other for one reason or another, but we always know that we are blood-related and nothing can come between us.

I believe that if at the end of life you can count your true friends on just one hand, you are blessed, much like the meaning of the word in W. B. Yeats's play *Beggars at the Waters of Immortality, or The Cat and the Moon.*

I had a long-time fascination with W. B. Yeats, culminating in my producing his play "The Cat and The Moon" at one of La Mama's theaters in New York. The aspect that intrigued me was his central theme of what we do in life; the choice, according to him, is between being cured of our afflictions, or blessed, meaning we accept our life as it is and live with it in understanding and love. I would have preferred Yeats to explore the situation further, but an audience will only sit still and absorb so much about a concept at one go, and perhaps he's right, for that one idea he communicated remains a guiding light for me, and I believe the audiences at his play understood the message and may even be nurturing it still.

The point of all the above quotes and writers, thinkers and actors who helped me to create my inner self is that the process is so complex in anyone's life that it defines each of us more certainly than a fingerprint. It is also our soul, and therefore is something very intimate and, hence, private.

I recently considered this because a friend in Hollywood read my latest book (*Out of Kenya, Out of Istanbul*, 2005), and suggested that he undertake to get a movie of it made. I thought about it for a day, discussed it with my wife, and declined because I consider a movie of my life and inner thoughts something over which I would have little or no control, and therefore it would become an unwarranted invasion of my privacy.

Saul Alinsky

He is little known, or remembered, today, but he was a strong influence on America in his day, and shaped my mind and soul in my formative years. He died years ago, in 1972, but trained and changed the thinking of thousands of ordinary people like myself, teaching us how to seize the initiative and radically change both our lives and those of people around us.

Saul's first book I read is *Reveille for Radicals* (1946). A few quotes will give you the idea: "An 'objective' decision is generally lifeless. It is academic and the word 'academic' is a synonym for irrevelant." And "A scared human being gives birth to a sacred cow." I read this just after World War II, in my early twenties, when I knew I was anti-establishment, but not why. I knew I was a liberal, but not really why. Saul informed me on both counts, and I thought I was also one of his radicals, for I liked what he wrote and did, but I lacked the guts to follow him into the streets and fight for my beliefs.

Like many in that era I was a vociferous advocate of civil rights, but I did not go to the American South and actually try to accomplish something. Saul wrote about me and people like me: "Liberals will settle for a 'moral victory'; radicals fight for victory." I never met Saul Alinsky, so I don't know whether he would have challenged my lack of radicalness, but I know he was right: we must fight for our beliefs.

Still, it's good to know I'm on his side, albeit somewhere in the safe background. Saul created what he called "People's Organizations" across the United States, which teach people how to organize and how to fight for their rights against industry, government, religion, or whatever was taking away the people's basic human dignity.

His last book, *Rules for Radicals* (1971), is best described by its subtitle, *A Practical Primer for Realistic Radicals*. He lived only a year after he wrote this book, but he was not softening his words. If you have not yet looked up the word *paraleipomena*, it's just a Greek word meaning things left out but now appended;

however, in this case, it's more accurate than either an epilogue, prologue, or prolegomenon, so I'll end with one of my favorite living authors.

Harold Bloom of Yale University

He has fascinated me since I read his authoritative *Shakespeare, The Invention of the Human* in 1999, and realized I found a replacement for A. L. Rowse, Oxford's distinguished Shakespeare scholar who had amused, insulted, and informed me for decades before his timely death. If you read any of Bloom's writings on Shakespeare, I think you'll be led to all his other books and articles, and especially my two favorites over this past winter (2006), *Jesus and Yahweh: The Names Divine*, which will both insult and excite you, especially if you're turned on by Bloom's challenge to think of the comparison of King Lear is to Hamlet as Yahweh is to Jesus.

If that doesn't challenge your fixed ideas, read Bloom's 2004 book *Where Shall Wisdom Be Found?* I was just finishing writing this book when I read his book and realized that he was writing the same book I was, only using different authors and coming up with different ideas and conclusions. Yet we are both on the same track, as his title indicates. The interesting aspect of his book is that the twelve writers he writes about are all writers I have studied and admired, but none of them appears in my book.

The point is that his presentation of each of his choices is so well thought-out and described that I was intrigued into buying a new copy of Montaigne's *Essays* in order to explore Bloom's thesis more fully. And that's really the point of reading books, isn't it? And then, to be able to change my mind about some aspects of Montaigne's thinking, and be able to write about that after I let it ferment in my mind for a few months or years.

Karen Armstrong

I cannot leave Karen Armstrong out of this bibliography, for her writing has been a mental firmament for me for a quarter century. Anyone who wants to know why they are here can find many of the answers in her sixteen books, ten of which I have in my library. She writes about her own early failures, such as her years trying to find herself as an English Catholic nun. Her curiosity about religion has brought her to be a recognized expert in Judaism, Islam, and Christianity, something very few have ever done before.

Her best book for a starter is *The Spiral Staircase: My Climb Out of Darkness*. Read that and you'll understand what real darkness is and how courageous her success is. Her latest book is *The Great Transformation. The World in the Time of Buddha, Socrates, Confucius and Jeremiah*. Or, as a *New York Times* review subtitles it: "The Beginning of our Religious Traditions." It's not as personal as the earlier book I mentioned above, but it's worth the time and trouble to learn about this period, roughly 900 BC to 300 BC, when religion per se achieved its basis as it is known today. I am so impressed with her writing, her research, and her thinking that I can almost forgive her for not allowing me to quote from her books during a play I produced in New York in 1997.

Rebecca Goldstein

Like Toynbee, I have asked many times why I am writing this book, and have answered in differing ways as my thinking grows. My final quote is from a new book by Rebecca Goldstein: *Betraying Spinoza*, published in 2006 by Nextbook. My impetus for buying the book was that Harold Bloom reviewed it in the *New York Times*, suggesting that I had too harsh a judgment of Spinoza and should think him through again, and especially reread his *Ethics*, a book I still find almost indigestible.

However, Goldstein's interpretation is lucid, despite too much writing about Jewish life and not enough about Spinoza. Toward the end, page 161, she cuts to Spinoza's heart and mind by writing that in his *Ethics* he makes the point that just proclaiming and supporting righteous deeds is not enough. "That would make being a saint too easy." "Our very essence, our 'conatus', will lead us, if only we will think it all through, to a vision of reality that, since it is the truth, is in our interest to attain, and will effect such a difference in our sense of ourselves that we will have trouble even returning to the prephilosophical attachment to ourselves."

I take the above to be a call to personal arms: to fight, not just to talk or write. Goldstein writes that Spinoza acted by reconstructing his own identity. She suggests that his new personal identity could not fit into "the terms of Jewish identity, nor of Christian identity, nor of any specific religious, ethnic or political identity." I interpret his concept as being close to my meaning as developed throughout this book, meaning that God can be identified with nature, or Nature, as exemplified by my oft-used quote: *Deus est mortale iuvare mortalem*, "God is a human helping another human."

978-0-595-41693-6
0-595-41693-4